MW00849953

"Every person who leads or is a member of a leadership team, or aspires to be, should read **Building Great Leadership Teams**. It is like a "cheat code" for how to build and sustain highly effective leadership teams."

Gil Brady, President Nativity Prep Academy of San Diego and co-founder of Relationship Impact

"I spent a long and diverse military career building teams of leaders. The work is never perfect but always worth the effort as strong teams enable the mission and protect lives. In **Building Great Leadership Teams,** Jack provides important principles and a practical approach for any leader aspiring to build a great leadership team."

General Robert Brown Ret., President & CEO Association of the United States Army (AUSA) and former Commander US Army Pacific

"Jack's experience and on-the-ground examples have created an insightful and pragmatic approach to building world class leadership teams. In particular, the path for CEOs to move from leading a senior staff to a true leadership team represents a real opportunity for many organizations. Building Great Leadership Teams is a great companion to any leader, whether new in their job or a seasoned veteran."

Mark Clouse, President & CEO of Campbell's Soup Company

"My company is living proof that the concepts and approach described in Building Great Leadership Teams work. Jack helped us move from a misaligned group of good individuals to a well-functioning leadership team."

John Goodwin, President & CEO of Goodwin Brothers Shades & Specialties

"**Building Great Leadership Teams** is the missing instruction manual for leaders struggling to get the most from their teams."

John Jantsch, author of 5 books including The Ultimate Marketing Engine; Founder of Duct Tape Marketing

BUILDING GREAT LEADERSHIP TEAMS

BUILDING GREAT LEADERSHIP TEAMS

A PRACTICAL APPROACH FOR UNLEASHING THE FULL POTENTIAL OF YOUR TEAM

Jack McGuinness

JONES MEDIA PUBLISHING

Building Great Leadership Teams
A Practical Approach for Unleashing the Full Potential of Your Team
Copyright © 2022 by Jack McGuinness

All rights reserved. No part of this publication may be reproduced, distributed, or transmitted in any form or by any means, including photocopying, recording, or other electronic or mechanical methods, without the prior written permission of the author, except in the case of brief quotations embodied in critical reviews and certain other noncommercial uses permitted by copyright law.

Disclaimer:

The author strives to be as accurate and complete as possible in the creation of this book, notwithstanding the fact that the author does not warrant or represent at any time that the contents within are accurate due to the rapidly changing nature of the Internet.

While all attempts have been made to verify information provided in this publication, the Author and the Publisher assume no responsibility and are not liable for errors, omissions, or contrary interpretation of the subject matter herein. The Author and Publisher hereby disclaim any liability, loss or damage incurred as a result of the application and utilization, whether directly or indirectly, of any information, suggestion, advice, or procedure in this book. Any perceived slights of specific persons, peoples, or organizations are unintentional.

In practical advice books, like anything else in life, there are no guarantees of income made. Readers are cautioned to rely on their own judgment about their individual circumstances to act accordingly. Readers are responsible for their own actions, choices, and results. This book is not intended for use as a source of legal, business, accounting or financial advice. All readers are advised to seek the services of competent professionals in legal, business, accounting, and finance field.

Printed in the United States of America

ISBN: 978-1-948382-35-9 paperback
JMP2022.4

CONTENTS

FOREWORD

Many years ago, when I began my first career in construction and decided to become a general contractor, the first overwhelming challenge I faced was building a team - it takes some 35 subcontractors and suppliers to build a house. Coordinating those companies and their leaders is the key to producing a project on time and on budget. Many lessons were learned along the way.

Twenty-five years later I brought those developed skills to my second act when I founded what is now ConnectOne Bank. The many iterations of going from denovo to an established public company required a deep understanding of not just good leadership, but rather the leadership qualities of a team.

We met Jack at a crucial time in our development and his work has been instrumental in getting our team to places we could have only imagined in a parallel universe.

Building a successful team is about thinking outside yourself, believing in a higher purpose, getting the benefit and the satisfaction of gaining the fullest potential of your team members along with seeing your organization grow to heights that to outsiders seem improbable or even impossible.

It has been most gratifying to see our company-wide results improve, our team members become better executives and to see a well-coordinated team function to take on the challenges that we face in a fast-paced environment.

My hope is that you will learn some of those lessons by absorbing the stories contained here.

Frank Sorrentino III, Chairman & CEO ConnectOne Bank

INTRODUCTION

I am in awe of the fortitude and perseverance that it takes to run a successful enterprise. The challenges are never-ending, and the failure rates are scary but, somehow, smart and driven folks figure out how to flourish. This book focuses on the collection of folks who lead these successful organizations – the leadership team – and the role they play to help their organizations grow and thrive.

Building Great Leadership Teams, demonstrates that a leadership team is a unique entity that can and should serve as an accelerator for your organization. You will learn what a great leadership team looks like and how it feels to be part of one. Most importantly, you will become intimately familiar with the hard work and concrete actions required to build a great team, including creating a sound structural foundation and forming the intangible relational fibers that serve as the lifeblood of great leadership teams. You will also discover the distinct skills and actions required to lead a great leadership team.

I wrote this book after years of witnessing the unnecessary struggles I see organizations go through because of leadership team dysfunction, and the amazing transformation many others make by stepping back and focusing on building great teams. Don't get me wrong, the work is not easy--; but it is a great deal easier when an organization deploys a pragmatic approach. *Building Great Leadership Teams* offers comfort to leaders that, while there is no perfect leadership team, they don't need to live with the dysfunction that is holding their organizations back. The advice, relatable stories, and practical approach I offer in this book gives leaders confidence on their journeys to build truly great leadership teams.

In each chapter of this book, I provide a quote that provides the context for that chapter, real-life examples from client engagements, and sensible advice and approaches for building great leadership teams. The end of each chapter includes the key takeaways. Let this be your invitation to embark with me on this worthwhile journey of learning how to build a leadership team that will help your organization thrive.

CHAPTER 1: LEADERSHIP TEAMS ARE IMPORTANT

"No matter how brilliant your mind or strategy, if you're playing a solo game, you'll always lose out to a team."

- Reid Hoffman

Several years back, a good friend introduced me to Bob, the CEO of Metropolitan Contracting. My friend told me that Metropolitan was "growing like crazy" with the addition of several well-known general contractor customers and a larger regional footprint. A few weeks later over lunch I learned a bit about Bob's journey and quickly discovered that, despite Metro's great success, he was quite frustrated. Bob had started Metro out of his garage 12 years earlier, and over the past three years sales had doubled on the backs of Bob, his sales team, and a seasoned field team that delivered great work and service. Recently, however, Bob began to notice some concerning cracks in the armor – a few unusual customer complaints, several over budget projects, and the loss of a couple of the best company's best supervisors; not to mention increasing tension throughout the organization.

A call from the CEO of his biggest and best customer – "you guys are killing us Bob; you have to coordinate with the other contractors, so we don't have setbacks like last week" – finally got his attention. After reflecting on how things had gotten so bad so quickly, it dawned on him that he and his leadership team might be a big part of the problem. As CEO, Bob was addressing problems that his direct reports should be handling. His leaders were pointing fingers at each other and their respective departments rather than figuring out how to address important challenges, and leadership team meetings went on for hours without resolving anything.

To get Metropolitan back on track, we worked together to begin to build the leadership team his organization need and deserved. He admitted to his team that he was part of the problem and committed to working with them to get organized and disciplined, taking the time to repair fractured relationships and gain agreement on a new way of operating. After a month into the effort, Bob expressed two emotions. The first was regret: *"Why did we wait so long to get our team in shape?"* But the second was excitement: *"We are about to accomplish so much more than we ever thought was possible."*

More Than Just a Staff Function

Research by McKinsey & Company, a management consulting firm, suggests that executives are *five times more productive* when working as part of a high-performing leadership team than they are when working as part of an average team. The research also indicates that aligned leadership teams have a 1.9 times increased likelihood of having above-median financial performance.[1] Gallup and other employee engagement research firms continually point to effective leadership teams as key contributors to employee engagement. Leadership teams aren't just any team; the stakes are much higher. On leadership teams, members are not just responsible for their functions or business lines. Instead, they are responsible for ensuring that all aspects of an organization are working in sync towards the direction they set.

Unfortunately, many leadership teams are structured as senior staff groups where most formal business interactions are primarily between the CEO and his functional direct reports. Functional leaders gain an understanding of the strategic direction and negotiate departmental priorities with the CEO. Incentives are primarily tied to departmental goals and objectives, perhaps with an overall financial goal for the company. The senior staff structure is most visible in how a CEO and his direct reports meet. Monthly or bi-weekly meetings are organized as progress reporting and information sharing venues with minimal challenge and debate. Most importantly, while there might be a clear understanding of the organization's mission and strategic direction, there is limited to no focus on the important efforts that a leadership team should be working on together.

While the senior staff model can work, experience and research suggest that evolving to a leadership team model can serve as a force multiplier for the organizations they serve (see Figure 1). First, with a senior staff model the ability to leverage the experience, talent, and wisdom of senior colleagues is squandered and opportunities for greater innovation are lost. When smart people challenge, debate, and problem solve with a focus on what's most important leadership teams and their organi-

---

1 Scott Keller, *High Performing Teams: A Timeless Leadership Topic*, (Boston, McKinsey Quarterly, 2017), 1.

zations make great progress. Next, when priorities are established at a departmental rather than a cross-organizational level efficiencies are missed. When team members integrate and address the organization's most pressing issues together, they increase opportunities to innovate, coordinate, and deploy resources more efficiently. Finally, when an organization's most senior leaders collaborate on important priorities and hold each other accountable for collective and individual actions and behaviors, there can be a tremendous downstream impact throughout an organization.

Senior Staff	Leadership Team
• Individuals focus solely on functional roles	• Individuals balance enterprise and functional roles
• Meetings focus on progress reporting and information sharing	• Meetings are forward-looking, resolution focused and focus on what's most important
• Problems are resolved by individual functional leads and the CEO	• Priority opportunities and challenges are addressed and resolved by the team
• Goals and priorities are established by individual functional leads	• Goals and priorities are established by the team

Figure 1: Senior Staff vs. Leadership Team

Building and maintaining a leadership team is a challenging and complex endeavor that is magnified in today's chaotic business, political, and social environment. The pace of change in the world we live – rapid technology advances, increasing and changing customer demands, social and environmental pressures, a pandemic! – have greatly increased the complexity of growing a healthy and productive organization. The challenge of managing interdependent organizational units that must anticipate and respond to this complexity is beyond the capacity of any one individual to steer; it requires a team of leaders. Leadership teams are quite visible to employees and external stakeholders, and how they operate and behave is intensely observed and often emulated. Further, organizations are often run by leaders who set the tone with inspiring visions and values, but without a leadership team that is committed to these visions and values, it is extremely difficult to lead a productive and healthy organization. One client suggested that without this type of commitment he felt like he was pushing a 1000-pound boulder up a big hill. The bottom line is that the buck stops with leadership teams; knowingly or unknowingly, they create the conditions for their organizations to either thrive or flounder.

Impacts of Unchecked Dysfunction

Leadership teams work hard to shape visions that rally employees, shepherd the execution of strategies that set their organizations apart from competitors, and define values that form strong cultural foundations. Unfortunately, these efforts often fall short and frequently one of the main culprits is a dysfunctional leadership team. Many leadership teams fail to install and reinforce fundamentals such as role clarity, cadence, operating principles, trust, and accountability. These teams become much more than an annoyance; they actually hold their organizations back. This conclusion is supported by a Center for Creative Leadership study which revealed that only 18% of senior executives rated their teams as 'very effective.'[2] In the same survey, 97% of executives agreed that 'increased leadership team effectiveness would have a positive impact on organizational results.'[3]

Leadership team dysfunction doesn't happen overnight; rather it is like an insidious disease that chips away at the fiber of an organization. In

---

2 Alice Cahill, *Are You Getting the Best Out of Your Leadership Team*, (Greensboro, Center for Creative Leadership, 2020), 1.

3 Cahill, *Are You Getting the Best*, 1.

most cases it is not very hard to spot a dysfunctional leadership team. While certainly not exhaustive, the examples below shed some light on what happens when dysfunction goes unchecked.

Doing the Wrong Work. Focusing on holiday parties and brochure colors to seating arrangements and performance review templates... These are all *real* examples of distractions that have inhibited leadership teams from putting appropriate focus on competing and growing. For example, the executive team of a $100 million professional services firm spent hours at multiple meetings critiquing performance review templates in the face of massive customer concentration risk.

Duplicating Effort. Symptoms include departmental infighting, customer frustration, and productivity challenges. A large government contractor received complaints from several customers about having their time wasted with multiple sales calls from the contractor's different lines of business at different times. A customer executive commented, "Are you one company or three different companies?"

Repeating Mistakes. Indicators might include customer frustration, chips in the accountability armor, and operational delays. A $30 million construction contractor experienced multiple delays in transitioning to a larger and more modern warehouse designed to improve productivity and strengthen service. In frustration, the CEO shouted, "These delays remind me of the same issues we had when we installed the new financial system, and it is burning money and destroying customer goodwill!"

Increasing Relational Strife. Symptoms include turf battles among executives resulting in friction at the departmental level, executives focused on departmental performance at the expense of company performance, and incentives that create unhealthy departmental competition. A $75 million management consulting firm expected collaboration among their customer acquisition and customer maintenance teams but sales incentives promoted siloed efforts.

Fire Fighting. Symptoms include continual focus on the latest crisis, constantly shifting resources, and endless surprises causing employees to react and shift from stated priorities. The leadership team of a mid-sized community bank referred to their management approach somewhat proudly as "brute force leadership." They all seemed to focus and work together in a crisis but the long-term impacts of this brute force approach on the organization impacts were significant – burnout, low morale, and turnover. The leadership team also suffered as teammates began to point fingers and work at cross purposes.

Characteristics of Great Leadership Teams

There certainly is no perfect leadership team and all experience periods of dysfunction. But *great* leadership teams develop strong foundations that enable them to weather these storms and get stronger. Great teams believe they can tackle any challenge and accomplish any goal.

As an executive team coach, I have worked with the leadership teams of over 100 growing companies across a host of industries. At the start of each engagement, we ask team members to think about the best teams they have ever been on – sports, business, community – and to remember what it felt like to be a part of those great teams. Words like trust, communication, accountability, common goals, respect, and innovation make every list. What we enjoy most is the passion that surfaces when team members call out and add color to these words. The following phrases often emerge:

> *"We always had each other's backs even when things didn't go so well."*

> *"The path wasn't always clear, but we all knew where we were headed and were confident that we could get there."*

> *"Everyone pulled their weight; we just didn't want to let each other down."*

> *"When we screwed up, we didn't point fingers; we just fixed the problem and did our best to not mess up again."*

As I will discuss throughout this book, there are many factors that characterize great leadership teams. However, based on client discussions and observation, I believe that every great leadership team has four crucial characteristics: focus, synergy, simplicity, and resilience.

Focus on Results. Great leadership teams are laser-focused on their most important priorities. They manage conflict productively and can challenge and debate important issues without defensiveness or fear of retribution. Simply put, great leadership teams do not let trivial issues get in the way of what is most important.

Synergy. Great leadership teams operate as systems that have characteristics transcending those of any individual members. They recognize that their true value lies in the unique and complementary talents each individual brings to the team and their ability to harness these talents in the interest of a common purpose. They serve as vehicles to accelerate their organizations and accept that they set the tone for how their organizations operate and behave.

Simplicity. Organizational psychologist Ralph Stacey's definition of leadership emphasizes the skills great leaders need to embody in today's complex, fast-paced environment. Stacey suggests "great leaders have a greater capacity to live with the anxiety of not knowing and not being in control while interacting creatively and productively."[4] Great leadership teams use their collective strengths to embrace the complex challenges they face every day and they break down these challenges into manageable components.

Resilience. Great leadership teams adopt this military cliché: *No battle plan survives first contact with the enemy.* Today's dynamic environment requires leadership teams to proactively plan but always be prepared to adapt and adjust course. Leadership teams are never 100 percent aligned all the time, but great leadership teams have confidence in their ability to get back in sync and learn from their mistakes after inevitable periods of challenge and dysfunction.

A Model for Building Great Leadership Teams

To help leadership teams create a roadmap for creating a healthy and productive entity, I developed a simple leadership team effectiveness model as illustrated in Figure 2 below. The model includes two sets of interrelated factors which we often describe as "two sides of the same coin." Structural factors help leadership teams focus on and achieve business outcomes while relational factors help leadership teams main-

---

4 Ralph Douglas Stacey, The Emergence of Knowledge in Organization, (Journal of Complexity Issues in Organizations and Management, 2000), 23.

tain productive and healthy work environments. When these two sets of factors are working in sync, we have seen leadership teams achieve heights they never thought were possible.

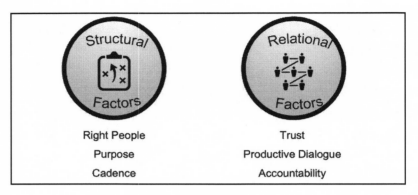

Figure 2: Leadership Team Model

A leadership team's structural foundation is the arrangement and organization of important tangible elements. Do team members understand their roles as *leadership* team members? Is there a clear purpose that defines what issues the team should be tackling together? Do team members address the natural gray areas between their roles? Does the team have a disciplined way of communicating, making decisions, and tracking progress? A well-thought-out structural foundation reinforces expectations, helps foster innovation, strengthens the quality of decision-making, and enhances cross-organizational collaboration.

While a leadership team's structural foundation provides clarity on *what* a team must do, its relational foundation centers on *how* the team behaves together. Relational dynamics are challenging enough in day-to-day interactions but are magnified when a group of talented senior leaders with different backgrounds, experiences, and approaches come together. Both sets of factors are critically important to the success of a leadership team, but relational dynamics serve as the grease that makes the engine operate well. When there is trust among a leadership team, it is much more likely to engage productively. When the team can challenge and debate constructively and members can hold each other accountable there is a greater chance that the team will be in sync on what is most important.

Structural dynamics and relational dynamics are inextricably linked. Growing companies often outgrow structure which can create confusion and put strain on relationships. The opposite is also true; relational challenges that go unchecked get worse, and any changes to structure often do not have the desired impact. Consider Metropolitan Contracting's situation discussed at the beginning of the chapter. Poor meeting discipline, functionally focused team members, and assumptions about gray areas between roles led to fractured relationships and Bob having to serve as the Chief Problem Solver.

The good news is that dysfunction doesn't have to define your leadership team. Don't expect that there won't be some dysfunction from time to time, but if you step back and devote time, thought, and energy into your team, it can become great. I am confident that the lessons and insights included in the following chapters will help you on this journey.

Chapter 1 Takeaways

1. Leadership teams have tremendous downstream impact on an organization and can either accelerate or hinder progress.
2. Many leadership teams are structured as staff functions where the emphasis is on the CEO and each direct report rather than the interaction and relationships among team members.
3. Great leadership teams (a) focus on results; (b) have synergy; (c) manage complexity well; and (d) are resilient.
4. A leadership team's structural dynamics and relational dynamics are inextricably linked.

SECTION ONE: STRUCTURAL FOUNDATION

CHAPTER 2:
GET THE COMPOSITION
RIGHT

"I can do things you cannot, you can do things I cannot: together we can do great things."

- Mother Teresa

A few years ago, I received a call from Phil, the CEO of a $100 million management consulting firm. He had just read an article I had written for Chief Executive Magazine and asked me if we could meet to discuss his situation. A week later I met Phil in his office, and he described his situation. Phil felt like he had picked 'A' players to serve on his leadership team but was concerned that the team was playing more like a 'C' team. The firm had a serious customer concentration issue with close to 70% of revenue coming from one client. Yet, while the team recognized the challenge, it was struggling to work together to identify innovative approaches that might set them apart from some formidable competitors. The solutions they developed lacked depth and failed to take into consideration the dynamic and competitive environment in which the firm operated. Meetings were dense and often devolved into discussions about current client challenges and disrespectful clashes about how to deploy resources.

Phil was concerned that he had selected the wrong leadership team members. The team lacked the discipline and ability to think ahead and the diligence required to address such a complex challenge. And the team's business unit leaders seemed unable to look beyond the needs of their units. Over the next few weeks, Phil and I developed a game plan to adjust course. Step one was to reset expectations about what it means to be a leadership team member at the firm. Phil settled on the following four characteristics:

1. *"On our leadership team, each team member has to think beyond today and continually evaluate the longer-term challenges and opportunities that may confront the firm."*
2. *"As we do in our functional roles, each of us must develop the ability to think past the obvious answer and be able to synthesize the volumes of information coming at us from multiple sources."*
3. *"As leadership team members, we are accountable to the firm first and then our business units"*
4. *"Our firm's values are essential to the health of the firm and each of us must model them in all of our interactions."*

Leadership Teams Aren't Like Other Teams

As I mentioned in Chapter One, leadership teams are not and should not be like any other team in an organization. Simply put, they create the conditions for organizations to either thrive or flounder. Because the stakes are so high, it is *critical* for CEOs to get the composition right.

Leaders at many companies rise the ranks in large part because of their past accomplishments and functional expertise; sales results for the head of sales, successful product launches for the CMO, balance sheet and capital raises for the CFO, technological innovation for the CTO. Advancement is also often a reward for putting in hard work and years of service or forming the necessary political bonds with the right senior influencers. Functional track record, work ethic, and political skills are necessary for any senior leader but are insufficient when a leader is asked to be part of an effective leadership team.

Great leadership teams establish and steer an organization's strategic direction and set the tone for how their organizations operate. In normal circumstances this is challenging work, but today's uncertain and complex environment requires leadership teams to be much more than a collection of talented senior leaders. To be successful, leadership teams have no other option than to leverage each other's talent so they can navigate the uncertainty in a manner that fuels innovation, enables operational agility, and inspires confidence.

So, what does it take to be a great leadership team member? In my experience, and in speaking with many CEOs, there are five unique skills that all senior leaders must have or at least be working to develop to be great leadership team members. These skills include curiosity, foresight, management of complexity, a greater good focus, and modeling values.

Curiosity. Leaders often progress in organizations based on their specialized technical talent – marketing, sales, strategy, engineering, etc. – and the experience they derive from excelling in these areas. Unfortunately, this talent and experience and the desire to project confident expertise is often what gets in the way of leaders being effective leadership team members. How many times have we seen a colleague stifle dialogue about a new idea or a particular way of doing business by referring to his 30 years of experience and the fact that he has seen it all?

A PwC survey of more than a thousand CEOs cited curiosity and open-mindedness as leadership traits that are becoming increasingly critical in challenging times.[5] Simply put, without curiosity leadership team members will hold their teams back. Great leadership teams are comprised of leaders who are constantly expanding their perspective and what they know without relying *only* on their expertise and experience. When faced with ideas that differ from their own or those that might even seem stupid or crazy, curious leaders ask questions and genuinely listen. "Tell me more about how that might work. How do you think that could apply to our business?" When embarking on a new initiative, curious leaders are inquisitive and seek the opinions and perspectives of others. Curious leadership team members promote more meaningful connections among teammates and help generate more creative outcomes for their teams.

Foresight. Today's leaders live in a world filled with volatility, ambiguity, and complexity. They are constantly challenged with staying focused on the future while facing the urgency of managing the day-to-day. According to famed futurist Richard Slaughter, foresight is "the ability to create and maintain a high-quality, coherent and functional forward view, and to use the insights arising in useful organizational ways."[6] Foresight is not about predicting the future. Rather, it is an important capability that helps leaders manage, harness, and leverage the constant change around them. It includes being able to sift through large amounts of conflicting information while being an astute observer of the environments in which they operate. Foresight helps leaders to anticipate challenges and to avoid letting situations dictate and overwhelm their organizations. To develop good foresight, leaders must be

---

5 PwC, 18th *Annual CEO Survey: A marketplace without boundaries? Responding to disruption*, April 2015.

6 Richard Slaughter, *The Foresight Principle*, (Westport, Praeger, 1995), xvii.

curious about learning and experimenting, disciplined about not letting their own biases get in the way, and passionate about engaging and learning from others.

Simplifying the Complex. Members of great leadership teams can break down complex information into logical patterns that enable simple solutions to emerge. In his "Simplifying Complexity" TED Talk, Eric Berlow suggests that 'the more you step back and embrace complexity the better chance you have of finding simple answers, and it's often different than the simple answer that you started with.'[7] On a leadership team, members must go beyond managing the complexity of their functional responsibilities and work together to manage complex cross-organizational challenges facing the entire organization. Simplicity matters because it has such a big effect on a leadership team's ability to communicate as a team and with the entire organization. Leadership team members who are not skilled at simplifying complexity hold their organizations back as they tend to lead reactive and inefficient functional units, ultimately contributing to confusion and frustration throughout an organization.

To begin to master the art of simplifying complexity, leadership team members must work on two important skills. The first is the ability to gather or observe complex data, identify the outcomes the team is trying to influence or evaluate, and identify patterns or interdependencies between the data– all in the interest of discerning potential conclusions or solutions. The second skill is the ability to communicate complex topics in a manner that satisfies the needs of recipients. This often requires prioritizing what's most important from the recipients'

---

7 Eric Berlow, *Simplifying Complexity*, (TED Talk, 2010).

perspective, articulating clearly and concisely, and providing context and examples.

Greater Good Focus. Being a productive member of any team is hard work and the challenges are exacerbated on leadership teams where egos, ambitions, and ingrained ways of working are often considerable. For a leadership team to be great, each member must think as CEOs do and be loyal to the team first. This requires team members at times to subordinate their functional or business lead role to that of the team. Leadership team members also need to gain a deep understanding of the broader strategic goals of their organizations and participate in trade-offs between different departments. For example, a CMO might make the difficult choice to support the hiring of additional software engineers at the expense of a digital marketing campaign.

This greater good focus is not always a natural skill and must be continually reinforced individually and collectively. Leadership teams need to actively discuss and gain agreement on the behaviors that support a greater good focus: "we" instead of "I", volunteering to give things up, and excitement about company success not directly related to their function. Team members also need to welcome and encourage input from their colleagues, even on topics outside of their expertise. Perhaps most importantly, all team members need to consistently model these behaviors and hold each other accountable to them.

Modeling Values. Values should not be just words listed on a website or posted in conference rooms. To find out if values in your organization have meaning, ask an employee in the breakroom if the posted values are real. If the response is "if you heard how the COO talks to his team you would laugh at our people first value" then you know there is work to be done. However, if the response is "heck yea, let me tell you how we take care of employees at this place," you can be sure that the leadership team is reinforcing these important behaviors.

Values should be the guideposts for how all employees in an organization behave. They will be consistently practiced across the organization only if every member of the leadership team works hard to model them in how they interact with all stakeholders, how they make decisions, and how they operate their individual units. Employees take their cues from the leadership team – service focus is diminished when a leader publicly disparages a customer, people first is diminished when a leader yells at a team member, and team focus is diminished when employees hear leadership team members speak poorly about colleagues.

Members of great leadership teams recognize that it is a privilege to be on the team. They may not be able to practice all the characteristics described above when they first join a leadership team, but they must have the capability to develop these important skills and actively commit to do so. Unfortunately, some functional leaders are simply not suited to be on a leadership team. They may be great technical contributors and do an effective job in driving their functional teams, but they might never be able to focus beyond today's challenges or manage complexity beyond issues in their technical domain or have a mindset that puts the organization's needs ahead of those of their function. These types of team members hold their leadership teams back and create unnecessary chaos. For example, the CTO of a cyber security firm continually wastes the leadership team's time with deep dives into technical challenges on projects and fails to listen to the perspectives of his colleagues when the team discusses important cross-organizational challenges such as addressing challenges with a core system or process, or implementing a new performance management approach.

Adding New Team Members

Research suggests that 40% of new leaders fail in the first 18 months on the job and that the estimated cost of exiting a new leader in this time frame is roughly three times the leader's first year salary.[8] Promoting a talented performer or hiring an experienced outsider to a leadership team are not trivial issues. The approaches run the gamut from telling the new leader to show up at the next leadership team meeting with little preparation to a formal onboarding program run by human resources. While the latter typically has a bit more success, even such methods can be flawed.

Over time, every leadership team establishes a unique character which makes adding new team members a challenging endeavor. This is not to suggest that the team development process must start from scratch every time a new member is added but it does suggest that focus needs to be put on incorporating new leaders in a manner that retains the essence of the "old" team personality while recognizing that a slightly "new" team personality will emerge. Perhaps the most important advice we can give to a team that is adding new members and potentially losing old ones is to listen and be open, be patient, and recognize that the team personality is going to change. Below are a few suggestions for adding new members.

Align. Great teams are aligned strategically (where are we going?), operationally (how are we going to get there?), and culturally (what behaviors will underlie our success?) and are resilient. It is a gift to help a new team member understand not only how the leadership team is aligned at each of these important levels but also to help this person to

---

8 Anne Fisher, *New Job? Get a Head Start Now*, (New York, Fortune, 2012), 1.

understand the struggles the team went through to become aligned. For example, if it took a good bit of time for a few individuals to establish the trust necessary to confront each other without defensiveness then the team should share this with the new executive so he can begin to gain some important insights into the team's dynamics. Providing a new team member with an opportunity to understand the rationale behind the team's alignment not only helps him to learn, but it also provides the entire team with an opportunity to engage the new team member on substantive issues and to challenge and the team's thinking.

Calibrate. Regardless of how well the promotion or hiring process is performed and how good of a fit a new leader might be, she is still an outsider as she enters her new leadership team. Biases are a natural part of human relationships and all parties involved will inevitably make assumptions. Specifically, new leaders often come to their new teams with preconceived ideas about the individuals on the leadership team and about how the team functions, and existing team members will have preconceived ideas about the new team member based on her previous role or the company she came from. While not easy, the trick is to call this challenge out and ask all parties to suspend judgment and take a fresh and open perspective to building new relationships. Psychometric instruments, like Strength Deployment Inventory® (SDI), can be great tools for accelerating the work of integrating new team members.

Educate. Another important step in acclimating new leadership team members is helping them understand the team's current behavioral norms (e.g., it's okay to challenge the CEO, we start and end our meetings on time, thorough preparation is expected) and management rhythm (e.g., our strategic reviews are quarterly, we review go-to-market execution monthly, operational updates are handled on our Monday morning calls). The addition of new team members is also a great time to evaluate norms, adjust the management rhythm, and engage the new team member to provide a new and fresh perspective. Even if little to no change is made, this has the effect of making the new team member feel like the team welcomes their input and that he can have an impact on the team even early on in his tenure.

Chapter 2 Takeaways

1. Leadership teams aren't like any other teams; they not only set and drive direction, but they also set the tone for the rest of the organization.

2. Great leadership teams consist of team members who know what it takes to be a valuable member (curiosity, foresight, complexity management, greater good focus, model values) and who either have those traits or are aspiring to develop them.

3. The character of leadership teams changes when members leave and new members are added. For this reason, it is very important to step back and recalibrate the team including – roles, and behavioral expectations.

CHAPTER 3:
DEFINE THE PURPOSE

"Individual commitment to a group effort: That is what makes a team work, a company work, a society work, a civilization work."

– Vince Lombardi

I had last worked with Maggie when she was a star SVP at a mid-sized government contractor. Three years into her run as founder and CEO of a growing cybersecurity company, she engaged me to help "build a strong leadership team that can help us scale." Like many CEOs at this stage, she was beginning to question her abilities as she watched her leadership team struggle. The team was filled with strong players who were passionate about the firm's mission and each member had played a part in shaping the strategic direction but, as Maggie put it, "we seldom seem to be in sync." As an example, Maggie recently discovered that her three sector VPs had called on the same high potential government agency to deliver three different pitches. She also observed that bi-weekly leadership team meetings were dense and usually devolved into addressing urgent project level issues or trivial issues such as what snacks to offer in the break rooms. Perhaps most frustrating was a gut feeling that while each team member was energized and fully committed to their functional roles, they seemed to place little importance on the team as a whole.

To begin to tackle the challenge, Maggie and I developed a list of probing questions to address with her leadership team. *Why are we tripping over each other? Why are we making inconsistent progress on our strategic initiatives? Why are our meetings so stale? Why are many of you lobbying me for your pet projects? Why does our staff seem confused about what's most important?* Clarity came when one team member boldly stated, "I don't even know what this team is supposed to do other than meet weekly to report progress to you." We all learned a great deal from these discussions, but the most important revelation was that the team was getting in its own way mostly because it had no idea what it was supposed to do together. After several weeks of intense discussions about the firm's most important priorities and the interdependencies among each team member's span of control, Maggie defined a focused and clear purpose for her leadership team: "For the next 18 months, our purpose will be to build an infrastructure (systems, processes) that will enable us to double in size in three years."

A Missed Opportunity

Many leadership teams do a good job of creating compelling missions, visions, and strategies that help their organizations execute. Some deploy structured planning processes and others use more intuitive, less formal approaches, but most fail to define the leadership team's collective role in executing a strategic direction. When we ask members of leadership teams to articulate their team's purpose, we often receive incredulous looks and statements like "our purpose is to carry out the company mission' or 'our purpose is to execute the firm's strategy." Mission and strategy are important components of a leadership team's purpose but as I will illustrate below, they are not sufficient.

Several things happen when a leadership team fails to define its purpose beyond mission and strategy. First, leadership team members naturally focus on the parts of the strategy that relate to their areas of responsibility, often without adequate consideration of other units. As an example, executives team members of a firm with a customer concentration problem approached the challenge in silos and without regard to the input from and impacts on their colleagues. Well-intentioned attempts to address an organization's priorities with a unit focus miss the opportunity to leverage the collective experience and talent of each leadership team member and fail to provide necessary integration from the organization's most senior leaders. The downstream impact can be quite consequential as nuanced differences in how individual team members speak to organizational priorities often result in confusion and units working at cross purposes. Finally, when leadership teams lack purpose, the time they spend together tends to be focused on reporting and sharing information rather than collectively addressing the firm's most important cross-organizational priorities. Inevitably, the work of the leadership team is seen by team members as less important than their individual efforts.

Lack of definition and clarity about a leadership team's purpose can also make it challenging for CEOs to select among competing organizational priorities. They fear that selecting the wrong priorities risks setting the organization back and selecting too many priorities might detract team members from effectively running their business units. Some CEOs also worry that defining purpose will surface disagreements among team members about the direction of the organization or which priorities are most important. Disagreements exist on any team, and they should be embraced on leadership teams, especially ones with talented and experienced members. Not having the discussions simply kicks the can down the road as the disagreements will no doubt emerge one way or another, and usually in a disruptive manner.

Shape a Compelling Purpose

Now that I have made the case for the importance of creating a leadership team purpose, let's discuss a few essential requirements for shaping a purpose that focuses and rallies the team and accelerates an organization. The first requirement is to ensure that the purpose is *important*; such as an acquisition, a serious competitive threat, restructuring, shoring up infrastructure, or retaining talent. It is surprising how many leadership teams wind up addressing trivial issues such as planning the holiday party or designing the new office space. The stakes are just too high for leadership teams to spend so much time on these types of issues. A leadership team's purpose should focus on a limited number (one or two) of the organization's most significant priorities for a discrete period of time; could be 30 days, three months, or two years. For example, when a community bank began to outgrow its infrastructure – processes were poorly defined, systems were disjointed, roles and accountabilities were confusing – the CEO focused his team. "For the next 18 to 24 months, the leadership team will focus the organization on building an infrastructure that will enable us to scale in an efficient, secure, and compliant manner." Often, a leadership team's purpose is quite easy to identify such as when an organization is faced with an immediate threat (e.g., new competitor taking market share, significant loss of talent, loss of a big customer, etc.). Other times the purpose may not be as apparent and, in these cases, the best place for the leadership team to turn is the strategic plan as it will provide guidance on the organization's goals and overall direction. The team should evaluate the strategic plan and discuss the priority initiatives that will benefit from their collective talent and leadership.

Another important requirement for shaping a compelling leadership team purpose is selecting priorities that have a *cross-organizational impact*. Purpose should focus on broad initiatives that impact all or most areas of an organization rather than priorities that can be handled by a single organizational unit. For example, the membership VP of a midsized trade association took on an important initiative to overhaul the association's membership database. While essential to the work of her teammates, the leadership team felt that this initiative could be driven functionally with regular updates on progress. In contrast, the leadership team of a $75 million management consulting firm decided that for the next 18 months its primary focus would be to lead the firm's effort to add new high revenue customers to reduce customer concentration risk by 20%. The team believed that together they could accelerate progress by first identifying the interdependencies among business units and then creating a coordinated plan of attack – a consistent go-to-market approach, an innovative approach to recruiting and training resources to work across business lines, and a financial plan to invest in the new approach. Shaping an important purpose with a cross-organizational focus helps to leverage the talents and experiences of each team member and galvanizes a team to work together.

The third requirement for creating a leadership team's purpose is *clarity*. This might seem like an obvious condition but sometimes it can be difficult to be clear. Often, a purpose is too broad because the team is trying to appease competing voices. Other times the challenge the team is facing is so difficult that it is hard to articulate a clear statement of purpose. To qualify as *clear*, a leadership team purpose should present the challenge (too much revenue from one customer), identify a goal (reduce concentration by X%), and provide a time frame (18 months). The following are a few insights for shaping a clear purpose that the team and the rest of the organization can understand. First, describe the purpose from the perspective of an employee without buzz words or vague phrases that have become a common vernacular of the leadership team. Next, don't avoid the natural disagreements that will emerge when smart, thoughtful people are asked for input. Finally, the CEO will sometimes have to use her authority to decisively settle on the team's purpose after hearing input from the leadership team.

A clear leadership team purpose that supports the organization's mission and strategic direction will help everyone strengthen their skills as effective leadership team members and will provide great context for influencing the cadence (the topic of the next chapter) the team uses to keep itself focused and organized.

Chapter 3 Takeaways

1. Mission and strategy are important components of a leadership team's purpose but are not sufficient for focusing the team on what issues they should be solving together.
2. A compelling leadership team purpose provides clarity to the team and the rest of the organization as it focuses on a limited number of an organization's most important cross-organizational priorities.
3. A leadership team's purpose should present the challenge, identify a goal, and provide a time frame.

CHAPTER 4:
CREATE A DISCIPLINED
CADENCE

"There is music wherever there is rhythm, as there is life wherever there beats a pulse."

- Igor Stravinsky

My first interaction with Capitol Construction's leadership team provided a telling picture. The recurring Monday morning meeting was supposed to start at 9AM and at about 9:10AM the CEO, Ted, got off his cell phone and frustratingly asked, "Where the hell are Cindy and Mark?" When the missing culprits finally showed up, Ted asked each functional leader to tell him "what is going on in your world." During these updates, which varied in substance and detail, it was clear that Ted was the only one paying much attention. He did get the team's attention a few times when he angrily shouted, "If you guys just talked to each other we wouldn't be having these setbacks." He then proceeded to tell them how to resolve the issues. After the individual updates, the team had a somewhat heated debate over the logistics for the annual summer staff picnic. The meeting ended abruptly when Ted answered his cell phone and the team drifted out of the conference room.

Ted and I went to lunch that day and, after asking me what I thought of the meeting, he interrupted and went on to tell me how frustrated he was. "I hate these meetings. We never seem to get much of anything accomplished, and we have some big challenges facing us." During lunch I was able to calm Ted down a bit and together we devised a plan of attack that would get the team focused on working together to address the organization's most pressing issues, and eventually help the team recognize and appreciate the importance of their time together. The key elements of the plan were focus and discipline focusing the team on the team's purpose and having the discipline (preparation, follow through, timeliness) to ensure that the team maintains this focus.

What Is Cadence?

Leadership team cadence is like the drum beat that helps a leadership team march in rhythm and alignment. More specifically, leadership team cadence is the *appropriate* pattern of interactions (meetings, one-on-ones, written communications) that *enable* a leadership team to shape, monitor, and adapt an organization's strategic intent. I emphasize two words in this definition. An *appropriate* pattern of interactions simply reflects the reality that context matters; there isn't a one size fits all cadence for every team in every situation. For example, during a crisis a CEO might take a more commanding and controlling leadership approach and adjust the team's cadence to meet and communicate more regularly so that increased visibility is given to those actions that will help the organization recover from the crisis. The word *enables* reflects that cadence is a facilitative tool and, while important, it is one of many tools that leadership teams use to effectively lead and manage their organizations.

A few years ago, I witnessed a highly effective cadence in action when I had the benefit of sitting in on one of the quarterly two-day leadership teamwork sessions of a rapidly growing $150M regional commercial landscaping company. Fifty plus leaders from across the region spent one day huddled with their lines of business colleagues (e.g., maintenance, installation, support, etc.) where they dug into their key performance indicators (KPIs) and challenged each other in sometimes heated but mostly improvement-focused discussions. The next day the entire team of leaders met in one conference room and presented their KPIs (pipeline, customer service, operating margin, etc.) and their plans for the next quarter to the executive team (CEO, President, CFO). Everyone came prepared, the agenda was clear, and the environment, while challenging, was supported by good humor and celebration. When I asked the CEO why he was willing to invest in these quarterly two-day events he said, "It's really pretty simple. We are a growing company with many moving parts and it is absolutely critical that all of our leaders speak a similar language, learn from each other, and recognize that we are all held accountable to reinforce the culture and drive performance."

Optimize the Cadence

By some estimates, the average leadership team spends less than three days together each month, and during that time they spend less than three hours on substantive strategic issues.[9] The price of this misused time is misalignment which often leads to faulty assumptions and less than optimal decisions. Cadence isn't a panacea for these challenges, but it is an invaluable tool for mitigating them. Gary Fussell, President of McChrystal Group, captures the essence of why emphasizing leader-

---

9 Michael Mankins, *Stop Wasting Valuable Time,* (Boston, Harvard Business Review, 2004), 2.

ship team cadence is so important. "Your rhythm should value purpose over habit, and effectiveness over efficiency. If...you are going through the motions, it's time to change it up. The purpose of your rhythm is to drive growth, focus, and unity as a group. If it's not doing that, then you need to change it up."[10]

To ensure the work of a leadership team moves from putting out the latest fires or dealing with trivial issues to maintaining focus on what's most important, the cadence it uses must be optimal. An optimal leadership team cadence reflects two important considerations – purpose and coordination. As we discussed in Chapter 3, great leadership teams have clarity on the important opportunities and challenges they need to address together versus those which can be handled by individual functional leaders and their units. The leadership team's purpose should dictate its cadence – who is leading and driving which initiatives, how often they need to meet, who should participate in which discussions, and the preparation and agendas for meetings. While issues related to the day-to-day running of the business should of course be part of the cadence they should not dominate.

Coordination is another important consideration for ensuring that a leadership team's cadence is optimal. Coordination of an operational calendar – shaping a strategic plan (annual offsite), monitoring, and reporting on progress (quarterly review of KPIs) and handling challenging operational issues (weekly check-ins) – is clearly an important part of a leadership team's function and it is what most teams focus on when establishing cadence. An operational calendar, however, is often not adequate for driving priority cross-organizational work. Additional coordination tools are required, such as project management discipline,

10 Gary Fussell, *High Performance Teams – Part 21 – Operating Rhythm*, (The Inner Chief Podcast, 2019)

cascading work teams, and an enhanced calendar. As an example, re-call the management consulting firm discussed in Chapter 2. The CEO rallied his team around reducing customer concentration risk by 20% in twelve months and used a few important coordination vehicles to drive results. These included a detailed project plan with accountabili-ties, milestones, and time frames; a cloud-based dashboard to track new customer wins; and weekly one-hour decision-making huddles with the leadership team and a few other key employees.

Manage Meetings Effectively

As discussed earlier, great leadership teams use meetings as important vehicles to support their cadence. Meetings help maintain coordination across functions and they also facilitate a team's ability to drive progress towards the team's specific purpose. On great leadership teams, mem-bers expect meetings to be time-bound, focus on what's most important, have clear agendas with expected outcomes and, when appropriate, to be full of lively debate, challenge, and resolution. For meetings to be most effective, team members must come prepared, actively participate, and hold themselves and their teammates accountable. Perhaps most importantly, team members should actively participate in discussions outside of their area of expertise and not get defensive when others en-gage in their turf.

There is no magic one size fits all formula for how often teams should meet or how they should track progress, but there are a few important guidelines. First, it is essential that leadership teams maintain discipline and provide adequate time for discussing and debating strategic issues separate from tactical issues. Too often we see teams set aside time to address an important strategic challenge only to watch the discussions quickly devolve into putting out the latest fire. If this becomes the team's default mode, then strategic execution will eventually suffer. Next, meetings are most effective when the heavy lifting happens in between meetings. The very best leadership teams handle a great deal of their work outside these formal settings in dyads and triads to maintain coordination and drive specific issues. Finally, it is important for leadership team meetings to be documented properly so that action items, parking lot issues, progress on metrics and plans are effectively monitored. While this might seem obvious, we often encounter teams that get together without an agenda and limited vehicles (i.e., parking lots, spreadsheets, dashboards) for keeping the team on track. These types of poorly planned and organized meetings tend to diminish team energy and hinder overall progress.

Operating Principles Facilitate Good Cadence

Being clear on what it takes to be a great team member, creating a compelling purpose, and establishing a good cadence are essential elements for building a great leadership team. But even with this foundation teams often struggle. By their very nature leadership teams are composed of individuals with different styles, backgrounds, and experiences so it is very important that they define, discuss, and gain agreement on the behaviors they expect from one another. We call these behaviors operating principles, but they are also often referred to as guidelines, commitments, or ground rules. Regardless of what they are called, these expected behaviors can serve as a valuable tool for accelerating a team's development. In the absence of operating principles, whatever behavior the team tolerates becomes part of how it operates; team members assume their own rules of the road and, unfortunately, the most unproductive behaviors become the norm (such as showing up late to meetings or talking over each other).

There are no hard and fast rules for developing operating principles. In some cases, a founding CEO might establish a first draft of the principles while in other cases more established teams might develop them based on what has worked in the past or based on challenges they might be facing with each other. Whichever method is used, the principles are much more likely to influence behavior positively if a team actively discusses, debates, and gains agreement on a limited and targeted set. Without attention, however, a leadership team's operating principles will emerge by default. Some principles will likely be constructive such as "team members actively participate in our meetings." while others may be less constructive such as "in our environment it's ok to be late or miss meetings." Context, self-awareness, and accountability are the keys to establishing and living by meaningful leadership team operating principles.

Clearly there are certain principles that will work for almost every leadership team (i.e., integrity, punctuality, etc.), but it is important for a team to be acutely aware of the context in which it is operating so it can create principles tailored to its needs. Some context questions might include: What are the unique business challenges facing the team at the current time? How long has the team been together? What are the different personality types that comprise the team? What have been their experiences working on other teams? Reflecting on context will help the team to shape principles that are relevant to their current environment.

Most leadership team operating principles emerge in response to a current or past behavior that one or more team members has perceived to be disruptive. Examples might include: "It drives me crazy when she goes off on tangents that aren't relevant to the agenda."; "I recognize that he is the CMO, but I'd like to hear what he has to say about these important operational issues."; "It is simply disrespectful to not respond to email messages that are directly relevant to the most important issue our team is facing." There is no doubt that every team member will have examples of similar frustrations and it is quite likely that these same team members will display behaviors that sometimes annoy their colleagues.

The process a leadership team goes through to agree to a set of operating principles can be a powerful vehicle for building trust and reinforcing the benefit of productive dialogue, which is the focus of Chapter 6. However, operating principles are only useful if all team members commit and feel accountable to following every principle all the time. Of course, we are all human so there certainly will be times when individuals violate the principles. What transpires when this happens is the real test! Great leadership teams don't rely solely on the formal leader to enforce operating principles; they constructively provide feedback to each other when principles aren't followed.

Chapter 4 Takeaways

1. Leadership team cadence is the appropriate pattern of inter-actions (meetings, one-on-ones, written communications) that enable a leadership team to shape, monitor, and adapt an organization's strategic intent.

2. A leadership team cadence is most effective (high participation, good outcomes) when it is squarely focused on the team's purpose.

3. Meeting management is another important vehicle for ensuring that a leadership team cadence is relevant and effective.

4. Clearly defined and practiced operating principles or expected behaviors are essential for executing a good cadence.

SECTION TWO:
RELATIONAL
FOUNDATION

CHAPTER 5:
GENERATE TRUST

"Trust is like the air we breathe. When it is present, nobody notices. But when it's absent, everybody notices."

- Warren Buffet

Recently hired to modernize a large health care trade association, Alex found his leadership team in shambles. Mid-level managers and staff were reluctant to share information with each other without first checking with the boss. Leadership team meetings were tense with executives subtly attacking each other. "I have asked Ted several times to work with me on this issue, but I guess he is too busy." Outside of meetings Alex began to feel like a referee on what felt like trivial issues with team members lobbying to take on high profile projects and attacking decisions made by colleagues.

Having worked together at his previous association, Alex asked me to work with him to get to the root of the issues. After I spent time with each executive, it became quite clear that the team felt like it had a trust issue. Some team members believed that others were in over their heads technically, and not doing a good job of leading their departments. Others felt that certain teammates always had excuses for why they couldn't keep commitments. One even went as far as to say that a few colleagues were "dishonest and would do anything to look good."

Recognizing that rebuilding trust is an uphill climb, Alex initiated a journey to repair trust that included a few difficult but important steps. He built substantive time into his cadence to enable the team members to get to know each other better. The team also worked to uncover and navigate similarities and differences in styles and beliefs, and to begin to give each other constructive feedback. Another important step was to learn how to address the often-faulty assumptions teammates made about each other that were getting in the way of trust. After several months, issues of trust certainly lingered, but Alex's team was beginning to feel like they had some helpful tools to navigate and continue to strengthen the trust fibers among individuals.

What Is Trust?

Trust is the fuel that helps leadership teams thrive. Without it, team members simply are unable to engage productively. Reinforcing this point are the findings from Google's seminal study on what makes a great team at Google: "Individuals on teams with high trust bring in more revenue, are less likely to leave Google, are more likely to harness the power of diverse ideas from their teammates, and are rated as 'effective' twice as often by executives."[11] Paul Santagata, Head of Industry at Google, puts it simply when he says, "There is no team without trust."[12]

---

11 Charles Duhigg, *What Google Learned in its Quest to Build the Perfect Team*, (New York, New York Times Magazine, 2016).

12 Duhigg, *What Google Learned.*

Trust is complex and has different meanings for different people, and it is usually emotionally charged. The dictionary by Merriam-Webster defines trust as the belief that someone or something is reliable, good, honest, and effective. or a reliance on character, ability, strength, or truth of someone or something.[13] After working with leadership teams of all kinds, I have boiled this definition into three important components: trust in competence, trust in character, and trust in dependability.

Competence. Trust on leadership teams isn't simply about the team members liking each other or enjoying each other's company. In fact, danger flares should go off on leadership teams where members are too nice to each other, and afraid to hurt each other's feelings, as this can be a signal that trust is fragile. Highly capable leadership teams consist of people who are competent in their roles, take pride in delivering quality work, and who constantly strive to be better. Members of high-trust leadership teams have high expectations not only for themselves but for others, and they welcome feedback. These teams strengthen trust by leveraging member's collective skills and abilities, seeking each other's input, sharing expertise and knowledge, and proactively offering support when teammates struggle.

Character. Character is a foundational dimension of trust. High-character leadership teams are composed of individuals with integrity, those who choose the right path even when it's more difficult. They are we-focused and consider the needs of the team as a higher priority than their own personal desires. Individuals aren't afraid to be wrong, readily admit their mistakes, and are committed to improving. They communicate directly, with curiosity, compassion, and empathy. On high-char-

---

13 "trust." *Merriam-Webster.com.* Merriam-Webster, 2021. Web. 28 October 2021.

acter leadership teams, when teammates fail to live up to commitments, colleagues don't rush to judgement and are able forgive and move on.

Dependability. Dependability is an essential trait of high-trust leadership teams. Team members work diligently to establish mutual expectations and rely on each other to live up to their commitments, whether completing an important task on time or being present at team meetings. Individuals take responsibility for mistakes or failures and communicate openly when confronted with challenges that get in the way of living up to commitments. This becomes natural over time as teammates demonstrate consistency and rationality in their actions and behaviors, as well as in the risks they take.

How Trust Diminishes

Great leadership teams don't happen by accident. It takes a great deal of effort, planning, communication, and a willingness to make things work for leadership teams to reach their potential. All leadership teams have flaws and experience conflict and, at times, even drama. The challenge is not to let these issues chip away at trust because trust is very difficult to repair.

In my experience, trust can diminish on leadership teams for a few reasons. First, teams tend not to spend the necessary time and effort to gain clarity on mutual expectations (i.e., roles, behaviors, operating principles). Trust can also diminish when leadership team members make assumptions based on their own personal views of the world rather than stepping back to gauge context. Finally, trust can be chipped away when teammates operate with what American psychologist Carol Dweck refers to as a "fixed mindset or a belief that an individual's qualities are fixed and therefore cannot change" rather than what she calls a "growth mindset or a belief that learning and intelligence can grow with time and experience."[14]

The Journey to Generate Trust

Great leadership teams are composed of talented individuals who come to their teams with a basket of technical skills, a depth of life and work experiences, and a diverse set of motivations and styles. These leaders manage success and approach stress and conflict with great variety. Some move from one win to the next with little celebration or acknowledgement. Many enjoy a good fight and can move on with no hurt feelings. Others struggle with the pressures of running a business and managing lots of people, and deal with stress by withdrawing or lashing out. These differences can be magical but given the natural variety of skills and styles it is not surprising that leadership teams often face relational challenges that chip away at trust and diminish the team's ability to engage productively.

Leadership teams often think of trust as an input when it's actually an output. Trust is an output of the individual and collective efforts to adopt a growth mindset and a reward for doing the work to build meaningful productive relationships. Generating trust is not a linear formula; it requires awareness of how we see ourselves and how others see us, plus a great deal of patience from every team member. Great leadership teams don't assume that trust will just happen; they take important steps that help to build a foundation of trust and recognize that, given the challenges of running a business, there will be times when

---

14 Carol S. Dweck, Mindset: *The New Psychology of Success,* (New York, Penguin Random House LLC, 2016), 6-7.

trust needs to be repaired. The following are three important steps for generating trust on leadership teams.

Get to Know Teammates at a Deeper Level. Given the fast pace and constant change in today's complex business environment, it is critical for leadership team members to know each other beyond functional roles and past experiences. Teammates must build deeper connections so that they can begin to appreciate the nuances that create understanding and establish greater bonds.

While social settings such as dinners, lunches, drinks, and other outings are helpful, setting aside even a small part of a team's cadence to establish a sense of curiosity and understanding among all members of a team can pay big dividends. To make the most of this time, teams should adopt what author Tasha Eurich refers to as the two sides of self-awareness: our view of how we see ourselves and our appreciation for how others see us.[15] Psychometric instruments such as the Strengths Deployment Inventory (SDI) are excellent learning vehicles and can be used to gain a deeper understanding of the styles and motivations of each team member. Exercises such as Patrick Lencioni's Personal Histories Exercise also serve as good tools to help teams gain a greater appreciation for why teammates view the world like they do.[16] If used effectively, these types of tools and exercises can have a tremendous impact. You'll often find people say things like, "wow, that explains a lot" and "now I understand why he approaches decisions in that way."

---

15 Tasha Eurich, Insight: *Why We're Not as Self-Aware as We Think, and How Seeing Ourselves Clearly Helps Us Succeed at Work and in Life,* (New York, Crown Publishing Group, 2017), 8.

16 Patrick Lencioni, *The Five Dysfunctions of a Team,* (San Francisco, Jossey Bass, 2002), 198.

The key for using tools relationship building and exercises effectively is vulnerability. According to Brene Brown, an expert on social connection, vulnerability lies at the root of social connection; it is the lifeblood of humility and can show up in many forms.[17] When teammates demonstrate that they are dependent on each other or when they admit to their mistakes, they are displaying vulnerability. Expressing our vulnerability tells the world we are human and serves as the grease for building good relationships.

Gain Agreement on the Importance of Trust. It is natural for varying levels of trust to exist among the members of a leadership team – some teammates may have worked together for years and can finish each other's thoughts while others may have had intense conflicts that have strained trust. Regardless of the situation, to build an environment of trust, leadership teams must discuss why trust is so important for their team. As discussed in Chapter 3, teams with a clear purpose get the trust building journey off to a good start because when individuals' interests are aligned, teammates are much more likely to build strong bonds that lead to trusting relationships.

Discussions like these require teammates to come prepared to listen actively to each other and seek to understand the perspectives of others who, in many cases, might have different views than their own. When we ask leadership teams what it means to have an environment of trust the answers vary greatly. Some may feel that "trust is all about getting the job done" or "it's obvious that we trust each other because we all get along," while others believe they "can trust someone if they are honest" and "trust is about not stabbing each other in the back." None of

---

17 Brene Borwn, *The Power of Vulnerability*, (TED Talk, 2014)

these perspectives are wrong but it's also important to understand a colleague's views when generating or repairing trust.

Beware of Assumptions. We all make assumptions to fill in gaps in what we think and perceive to help us make sense of a complex world. But left unchecked, assumptions can be dangerous and may lead to unintended consequences. One type of assumption is often referred to as the hangover effect. For example, despite a new CEOs hands-off, empowering approach some team members behaved as if the old CEO's micromanaging style was still present; Why is he asking that?, how come he provides so much detail in his email responses? Other assumptions are based on behaviors team members see from their colleagues, often related to competence. For example, someone may think a person has no idea what she's doing, simply because she asks too many questions and takes too long to get to the point during meetings. This certainly may be a development challenge, but it is not necessarily a question of someone's competence. Trust is generated when teammates take time to discuss the behaviors they are seeing that contribute to assumptions, digging deeper to understand the motivations and intent behind the behaviors. For instance, they may realize the person who asks a lot of questions is just very detail-oriented, always seeking to get to the best course of action.

As explained in the article, "The Problem with Assumption and the Power of Inquiry," the antidote to unchecked assumptions is *inquiry*.[18] When team members are curious about a behavior that seems odd, annoying, or disturbing, they should pause to reflect on other potential realities beyond their first reactions; often, new realities will emerge in

---

18 Patrick Malone and Ruth T. Zaplin, *The Problem with Assumption and the Power of Inquiry*, (The Public Manager Magazine, 2014), 44.

doing so. Team members must embrace the fact that they are often venturing into the unknown together and, as such, there will be times when assumptions about what will be discovered and acted upon do not hold up. Embracing Carol Dweck's growth mindset can help team members move beyond assumptions as illustrated in the graphic below.

Fixed Mindset Phrases	Growth Mindset Phrases
I can't trust them because they never keep their commitments.	Can we talk a bit about our expectations for each other?
I can't trust him because he's simply not good at his job.	Can we spend a few minutes talking about the work we do that has a mutual impact?
I don't trust her because she thinks she's always right.	I admire how you have such conviction. Would you be open to considering a few other options?
I don't trust them because they always point blame at us.	I recognize that sometimes we make mistakes. Would you be open to discussing how we might improve?
I can't trust him because he acts without considering impacts.	I admire your ability to take action. Would you be open to stepping back at times to discuss impacts?

Figure 3: Fixed & Growth Mindset Phrases

Chapter 5 Takeaways

1. Trust is foundational for building great leadership teams and consists of three important components: (a) trust in competence, (b) trust in character, and (c) trust in dependability.
2. To build trust, each team member must reflect on how they see themselves and understand how their teammates see them.
3. Leadership teams often think of trust as an input, but it is not; it is an output of the individual and collective efforts to adopt a growth mindset and a reward for doing the work to build meaningful productive relationships.
4. To build trust, leadership teams must take time to get to know and be vulnerable with each other, understand the similarities and differences of how team members view trust, and work hard to avoid often faulty assumptions about colleagues.

CHAPTER 6:
ENGAGE IN PRODUCTIVE DIALOGUE

"We have but two ears and one mouth so that we might listen twice as much as we speak."

- Thomas Edison

Several years back, I worked with the leadership team of a management consulting firm that was concerned about the firm's stagnant growth. After much reflection, the team realized it was putting too much emphasis on internal issues such as leverage, staff training, and decision rights and not enough on serving customers and growing its pipeline.

Through a few heated but constructive work sessions, the team agreed that it needed to stop churning and avoiding difficult discussions about market development. Instead, they need to begin to address important issues as a team rather than relying on the CEO to improve fractured relationships among teammates. The work certainly was not easy, but the outcomes were tangible. To start, it became crystal clear to the team that their primary focus had to be on market facing issues. Team meetings improved dramatically as they began to debate with less defensiveness, resolve important issues and move to the next, and coordinate business development initiatives more seamlessly. While the team had periodic setbacks, the members came to realize the importance of working to stay engaged productively so they could lead their very promising firm to its full potential.

What Is Productive Dialogue?

Productive dialogue is the ability for leadership teams to challenge, debate, and discuss their most important issues in a manner that progresses these issues and leaves minimal relational scars. Fostering productive dialogue is a rare practice in most organizations because it is natural for adults to want to avoid tough discussions. As highlighted in a recent Harvard Business Review (HBR) article, productive dialogue on some leadership teams is often thwarted by "political infighting, defensive behavior, or hidden agendas. Critiques of ideas often become critiques of personalities. Even more common is a culture of politeness where teammates minimize differences as opposed to amplifying them, in an effort to avoid conflict."[19]

Dominance	The CEO overpowers the team by pushing their own point of view without listening to other perspectives.
Elephant in the Room	There is a clear elephant in the room, but everyone just seems to skirt the potentially difficult topic.
Love Fest	Teammates are extremely complimentary to each other but clearly struggle to give constructive feedback.
Passive Aggressive	Ideas are knocked down indirectly or via subtle insults, direct confrontation is avoided, or people pout.
Lobbying	All appear to agree to a course of action but after the meeting individuals lobby the CEO about a different approach.
Turf Protecting	Regardless of the issue raised, teammates argue for what is best for their departments rather than what is best for the organization.

Figure 4: Symptoms of Non-Productive Dialogue

---

19 Linda A. Hill, Emily Tedards, & Tara Swan, *Drive Innovation with Better Decision Making*, (Boston, Harvard Business Review, 2021), 10.

Productive dialogue is one of the most important elements for building a great leadership team. It relies on a foundation of trust (as discussed in Chapter 5) and what American author and Harvard Professor Amy Edmondson refers to as psychological safety. In her landmark study on the science of teams, Edmonson coined the term psychological safety to describe "the shared belief that it's safe to ask one another for help, admit mistakes, and raise tough issues."[20] She goes on to suggest that "psychological safety is meant to suggest neither a careless sense of permissiveness, nor an unrelenting positive effect but rather a sense of confidence that the team will not embarrass, reject, or punish someone for speaking up."[21] Most importantly, Edmonson's research discovered that the highest performing teams were "the ones with the highest reported errors – teammates were comfortable openly discussing mistakes."[22] On these teams, members weren't afraid to tell the leader that something had gone wrong. Simply put, productive dialogue cannot occur without psychological safety. CEOs play a big role in establishing or reestablishing psychological safety on leadership teams by modeling productive dialogue. When CEOs demonstrate that they are open to feedback and actively listen to different perspectives, and view confrontation as a natural part of the team's way of operating, leadership teams are much more likely to engage more productively.

---

20 Amy Edmondson, *The Fearless Organization: Creating Psychological Safety in the Workplace for Learning, Innovation and Growth*, (Hoboken, Wiley & Sons, Inc., 2019), 8.

21 Edmondson, *The Fearless Organization*, 14-19.

22 Edmondson, *The Fearless Organization*, 10.

The Keys to Productive Dialogue

Productive dialogue enables teams to remain focused on what is most important and leverage the contributions of each team member so that creativity and innovation flourish, and challenges and opportunities are proactively addressed. Establishing an environment of productive dialogue is hard work. Below are the key elements for building an environment where productive dialogue can thrive.

Self-Awareness. All leaders have blind spots that sometimes hold them back from being their best as colleagues, bosses, or teammates; they think they are behaving one way while others see them showing up differently. Leaders are often shocked when they get feedback from colleagues (often for the first time). "What do you mean I don't listen?" "I don't let my direct reports off the hook." "I don't waffle when making decisions– I'm actually quite decisive!" To create an environment where team members proactively address their blind spots, team leaders need to commit to addressing their own first.

In her recent Harvard Business Review article, Tasha Eurich suggests that there are *two* types of self-awareness. Internal self-awareness represents how clearly we see our own values, passions, reactions, and our overall impact on others while *external self-awareness* relates to understanding how other people view us.[23] Eurich goes on to say that experience and power can hinder self-awareness. "Seeing ourselves as highly experienced can keep us from doing our homework, seeking disconfirming evidence, and questioning our assumptions." Both types of self-awareness are clearly important, but experience suggests that relation-

---

23 Tasha Eurich, *What Self-Awareness Really Is (and How to Cultivate It)*, (Boston, Harvard Business Review, 2018), 1.

ships among leadership team members are strengthened when each individual strives to understand how others view them, so they are not clouded by inaccurate assumptions and lack of diligence.

Good Intent. On great leadership teams, destructive behaviors aren't allowed to fester or get in the way of what's most important. When a teammate is down or unaware of how their behaviors are received by others, their colleagues help them out; they become the adult in the room this time (maybe next time they will need the same type of support). Team members react first by assuming good intentions and work diligently to read each tense or difficult situation; "Is it necessary to address this right now?" or "He must be having a bad day." When they *do* engage, they do so with empathy and curiosity; "I understand why you are frustrated but we all make mistakes. I am sure that together we can figure this out." I am in no way suggesting that being the adult in the room is *easy* but when team members focus on what's most important, they tend to rise above the natural relational challenges that exist on even the best of leadership teams.

Disagreement. Disagreements are an inevitable, normal, and healthy part of any leadership team. Unfortunately, many of us are not very good at disagreeing and, as a result, disagreement often turns into unproductive conflict (see sidebar on the perils of the Conflict Avoidance Dance). Team members either avoid disagreement for fear of being uncomfortable, wrong, or judged or enter discussions as if they were boxing matches with a "win at all cost" mentality. Learning how to disagree is a straightforward concept but the work is hard; especially if the team's experience with disagreement has been less than constructive. Learning to disagree well requires three things. First, you need commitment from both sides of a disagreement to be curious; each person needs to listen and really try to understand each other's perspectives. Next, both parties must try hard to shift from a 'disagreement is awful' mindset to a "we will figure this out" mindset. Finally, and most importantly, teammates must learn, reflect, and reinforce the positive feelings and outcomes they have when they experience productive disagreements.

* * *

SIDEBAR: The Conflict Avoidance Dance

Most adults do not like conflict. It makes us uncomfortable and increases stress, so we avoid having the tough discussions necessary to push important issues forward. We assume that others will be put off by our challenging their perspective, providing constructive feedback, or simply sharing a different view. Our past experiences with conflict and our sincere desire not to hurt others' feelings certainly inform how we view and deal with conflict. Unfortunately, many of us fall into an awkward rhythm I refer to as the conflict avoidance dance.

> *Someone says or does something I don't agree with. I get frustrated but don't say anything. My frustration grows and I passively and sometimes actively take it out on the other party. The other party notices my behavior and avoids rather than confronts me. The other party gets frustrated. Another triggering event happens (often trivial) which sets one of us off and we react emotionally.*

The problem with avoidance is similar to that of pushing on a balloon – at some point the balloon pops and the conflict escalates. The remedy for improving a leadership teams' ability to deal with tough issues is to talk about and establish some guidelines for managing conflict productively. Typical guidelines for evolving to a more positive view of conflict management include (a) providing feedback and observations in a respectful, forward-looking manner; (b) committing to be curious and open to other's perspectives; and (c) learning to disagree for the greater good of the team. Great leadership teams work hard to embrace and see conflict as a natural and important part of how the team operates.

* * *

Chapter 6 Takeaways

1. Productive dialogue is necessary for leadership teams to challenge, debate, and discuss their most important issues in a manner that progresses the issues and leaves minimal relational scars.

2. Without trust and psychological safety, productive dialogue on leadership teams is virtually impossible.

3. The keys to productive dialogue include (a) self-awareness, (b) assuming good intent, and (c) learning to disagree.

CHAPTER 7:
CREATE A DURABLE ACCOUNTABILITY FRAMEWORK

"On good teams coaches hold players accountable. On great teams players hold players accountable."

- Joe Dumars

As our dinner progressed, so did Helen's frustration. Helen was well into her second year as CEO at Lightning Government Services and she was tired, cynical, and beginning to question whether she was even the right person for the job. Despite attempts by her executive assistant, Helen's office was like a revolving door. After leadership team meetings, direct reports would stop by her office to question the decisions and actions of colleagues. Every cross organizational decision – from implementing critical compliance processes and resolving sensitive client challenges to making calls on which opportunities to pursue – seemed to fall back on Helen's shoulders. Lightning was beginning to make some big mistakes, including missing proposal deadlines and pushing up on its line of credit. Helen decided things needed to change.

During dinner, we dug into the challenge and Helen began to realize that she had inadvertently created a serious accountability problem. The next day she scheduled an impromptu leadership team meeting to address the challenge. She conveyed her frustrations to the team and made it clear that, while she was largely responsible for the accountability challenge, they all needed to make some changes. She clarified everyone's expectations; from leadership team members to her own role as CEO in supporting and driving specific areas. For example, the team agreed to refine the business development process so that responsibilities and criteria for moving forward or killing an opportunity were clearer. Her direct reports discussed their apprehension to question teammates but agreed that the team would be stronger if they could engage with each other more directly rather than relying on Helen to intervene. While this was a good start, they all realized that they had a big hill to climb.

True Accountability

In his HBR article, "The Best Teams Hold Themselves Accountable," Joseph Grenny suggests that the worst teams have no accountability, mediocre teams rely on the boss for accountability, and the best teams hold themselves accountable.[24] Teams without accountability churn on the same problems with no resolution and tolerate unproductive behavior like pointing fingers and throwing blame around. Additionally, teammates who don't feel responsible have nothing motivating them to perform at a higher level. Ultimately, when one or more team members aren't held accountable, it negatively affects the whole team.

---

24 Joseph Grenny, *The Best Teams Hold Themselves Accountable*, (Boston, Harvard Business Review, 2014), 1.

As illustrated in the example of Lightning Government Services, teams that rely on the boss to hold them accountable struggle to scale, as too much weight is put on the shoulders of the boss. Perhaps more alarming is the downstream impact that inadequate accountability can have on the rest of the organization. A study by AON highlights this challenge as it suggests that everyone in the organization is watching to see how leaders hold each other accountable.[25]

In recent years, a great deal has been written about accountability and creating cultures of accountability. *But what is accountability?* On some leadership teams the word accountability has a mostly punitive connotation and can be a source of shame and negative criticism. Reactive phrases like "if we are going to get out of this hole, we need to hold people more accountable" emanate, and rather than "light a fire in people" come across as condescending and deflating. Other leadership teams view accountability as a structural or administrative issue and rely on accountability charts and performance metrics to drive results and help determine rewards or punishments. The phrase "what gets measured, gets done" is prevalent on these teams and, while well-intentioned, this type of approach usually falls short of instilling true accountability.

True accountability on a leadership team is a personal value shared by all team members that goes beyond doing a job or achieving metrics. True leadership team accountability is a commitment to the team that each team member will do what they say, accept responsibility for their actions and outcomes, and proactively and constructively help each other live up to their commitments. Great leadership teams evolve into ones where individuals feel accountable to the team, the leader serves more as a coach rather than the primary source of accountability, and

---

25 AON Hewitt, *Global Best Practice Research Report*, 2012.

the team becomes competent at holding itself accountable. This optimal leadership team accountability construct is extremely difficult to establish and requires plenty of nurturing, commitment, and patience on the part of each team member.

Making Accountability Durable

Many leadership teams value team accountability but only a select few actually practice it. The pace and stresses of leading any organization puts pressure on relationships which are critical for maintaining team accountability. Under stress it is often easier to fall back on the CEO or to point fingers at colleagues rather than to take responsibility or confront teammates. The good news is that the journey to move leadership teams towards team accountability are worth the effort because they can take teams quite far. That journey relies on a few important elements that build on many concepts covered in the previous chapters, including modeling, managing expectations, clarifying structure, and giving/receiving feedback.

Modeling Accountability. One of a CEO's most important jobs is to create and enable an environment where their teams can thrive. Modeling accountability is paramount to this. A CEO must take responsibility for his actions and admit when he makes a mistake. He must work hard to not let his position of authority get in the way and avoid deflecting, shifting blame, or moving the goalposts. CEOs must also model receiving feedback with curiosity and a genuine desire to understand and provide feedback with a focus on helping individuals learn and grow. CEOs also need to clarify that their role does not exist to settle problems or constantly monitor the team; rather, their focus should be on creating an environment where teammates help each other and address concerns immediately, directly, and respectfully.

Managing Expectations. At its foundation, accountability requires discussion and agreement on mutual expectations. To assume that expectations will be clear without any discussion is a recipe for disaster (see sidebar on Making the Implicit *Explicit*). The CEO must make it clear that not only is it okay for teammates to hold each other accountable, but it is also part of the job of a good leadership team member. The team needs to shift the often-negative connotations of accountability and begin to view it as a vehicle for helping the team and each individual to make progress and get better. Team members also need to discuss their basic expectations of each other. A good starting place for this discussion are the great leadership team member characteristics presented in Chapter 2. *Do we act with curiosity? What does it look like to have a 'greater good' focus? What does it mean to manage complexity well? How does a team member demonstrate their foresight skills? How does a team live their core values?* Great things can happen when team members encourage and challenge each other to further develop these important skills. Reflecting on the leadership team's purpose, the subject of Chapter 3, will provide further clarity on the specific accountabilities of team members and their respective functional units.

Clarifying Structure. As described thus far, accountability is mostly about mindset and behaviors, but there are certainly structural factors that enable effective accountability. One very important structural element is the practice of assigning responsibilities, scope, and time frames for important initiatives. It might sound basic, but I have seen too many leadership teams churn on the same issues over and over by failing to assign responsibility for key initiatives, not taking time to clarify scope and expected outcomes, and neglecting to determine key milestones and end dates. Another structural factor that can greatly enable accountability is incorporating progress reviews into a leadership team's cadence. By itself, this simple tool shines a spotlight on a team's expectation to make progress and learn lessons.

Giving and Receiving Feedback. As indicated by Professors DeNisi and Kluger in an Academy of Management Executive article, one of the most widely accepted principles in psychology is the positive effect that feedback has on performance.[26] Despite this convincing principle, experience suggests that one of the most challenging aspects in building a great leadership team is the inability of team members to give and receive feedback well. Without feedback, accountability is virtually impossible. Leadership teams that take the time to build trust and create an environment of psychological safety are much more adept at feedback; teammates are less likely to feel judged and more likely to recognize good intent.

Leadership teams further enable accountability by discussing and practicing principles for giving and receiving feedback. There are three important principles for giving effective feedback. Start by recognizing and being receptive to the fact that your feedback could be wrong or inaccurate. Next, be respectful and use a constructive tone and language to deliver feedback so that you are more likely to be heard. Finally, focus more on what you are hearing than what you are saying. There are also three principles for receiving feedback. First, demonstrate in your tone and body language that you are listening by hearing what is being said rather than just thinking about how you are going to respond.

---

26 Angelo S. DeNisi and Avaham N. Kluger, *Feedback Effectiveness: Can 360-Degree Appraisals be Improved,* (The Academy of Management Executive, 2000), 129.

Next, maintain a sense of curiosity when receiving feedback, even if you believe the feedback is wrong or confusing. A phrase like "tell me more" can be magical as it demonstrates your openness to hearing another perspective. Finally, be appreciative and thank others for taking the time to provide their unique perspectives.

* * *

SIDEBAR: Make the Implicit *Explicit*

During a client leadership team work session, an insightful team member used the phrase "let's make the implicit explicit!" A simple phrase and practical advice, but many leadership teams struggle to make being explicit part of how they operate. *Why is being explicit so difficult?* The following are some observations pulled directly from client interactions. First, we often assume clarity exists when it really doesn't. "He plays a global functional role so he clearly will ensure that all regions are well-coordinated." Next, sometimes it's easier to be a bit ambiguous rather than debate different points of view. "I know he thinks he owns that project, but I actually own it so, rather than argue, I am going to just behave as if I do and see what happens." Finally, many times the rules of the game (roles, processes, policies) either don't exist, are articulated poorly, or don't reflect the current environment.

It is obvious that a lack of clarity can wreak havoc on a leadership team; team members and departments duplicating efforts or working at cross-purposes and growing frustration often chips away at trust. Here's an approach for increasing clarity on your leadership team. First, if clarity seems to be an issue, then someone needs to have the courage to call it out and see if the team agrees. If team members agree, then they need to commit to working on making the implicit explicit. "We commit to asking the next question of each other to make sure we have clarity when something seems vague." Finally, when leadership teams trip up and discover that things weren't as clear as they thought, individuals need to assume positive intent and work together to gain clarity.

* * *

Chapter 7 Takeaways

1. Many leadership teams value team accountability but only a select few actually practice it. It is the journey to move leadership teams towards team accountability that can take teams quite far.

2. True leadership team accountability is a commitment to the team that each team member will do what they say, accept responsibility for their actions and outcomes, and proactively and constructively help each other live their commitments.

3. There are four important concepts for helping leadership teams build true team accountability: modeling accountability, managing expectations, clarifying structure, and giving and receiving feedback.

SECTION THREE:
HOW TO BUILD A GREAT
LEADERSHIP TEAM

CHAPTER 8:
THE TEAM LEADER'S ROLE

"What you do has far greater impact than what you say."

- Steven Covey

"I don't think I want to keep doing this, Jack." This is the response I received from Jeff after asking him *what* was getting in the way of him living up to the commitments he had made to his leadership team. Jeff was the CEO of SciStaff, a growing staffing company for medical research organizations. He had hired me to help "get his team in shape" to scale. A month earlier, the team came away from a half day work session energized by the commitments they made to each other to strengthen their leadership team. They included assuming good intentions, closing the communications loop, listening to other perspectives, and coming prepared to meetings. While some team members were struggling, all but Jeff were trying hard to live up to their commitments. Jeff continued to give multiple team members the same task, listen to the loudest voice, and deflect blame; and the team was becoming frustrated and deflated.

Six months later, I discovered that the chief operating officer and human resources VP and several other employees had left with great frustration; the business development VP, the loudest voice, was promoted to COO.

The CEO Needs a Leadership Team

Most senior executives agree that the complexities of running an organization have increased. Continuing technological innovation and an abundance of real-time information have intensified already increasing pressures from customers, competitors, regulators, and other stakeholders. This complexity coupled with the fact that an organization's activities must be well-coordinated and aligned broadly and deeply has made leading any organization today a challenging endeavor and way beyond the capacity of any one individual. To emphasize this point it is worth repeating the quote at the beginning of Chapter 1 by Reid Hoffman-- "No matter how brilliant your mind or strategy, if you're playing a solo game, you'll always lose out to a team."

To address this challenge, many contemporary organizations rely on leadership teams consisting of the CEO and her direct reports. Unfortunately, experience and data suggest that leadership teams often fail to live up to their potential. Recall the Center for Creative Leadership survey referenced in the first chapter where only 18% of senior executives rated their team as "very effective," while 97% agreed that "increased effectiveness of my executive team will have a positive impact on organizational results."[27] Simply put, building a strong leadership team is important and requires a talented CEO who can create the proper conditions for her team to thrive.

---

27 Cahill, *Are You Getting the Best*, 1.

The CEO's Role

As mentioned above, the CEO's primary role is to establish the conditions that will help her leadership team thrive. Unfortunately, the work isn't simple and is often made more challenging by the tendency of many executives to assume that with experience and position comes the ability to serve as an effective leadership team member. Evolving a group of executives, even highly skilled and talented ones, into a cohesive unit that points the organization in the right direction is a complex endeavor that requires time and nurturing. This hard work involves five very important commitments, described below.

Determine Composition. As important as shifting a leadership team's focus from staff-oriented to team-oriented is how a CEO chooses to comprise the team. Typically, CEOs select their direct reports who run functions or business lines to be part of their leadership teams. In other cases, CEOs might add senior managers they believe will add value to specific issues the team needs to tackle. For example, an HR VP who reports to a COO might be included if acquisitions are a key part of the team's focus.

Regardless of the types of roles a CEO chooses, there are two critical actions she must take to ensure the composition is most effective. First, while it might sound like a nuance, the message a CEO sends when inviting team members to participate is crucial. Team members must be invited with the primary purpose of leading the organization and not just representing their respective units. If this is left unstated, most team members default to advocating primarily for their functional or business line interests at the expense of what is best for the whole. Second, CEOs must set clear expectations that each team member must possess – or at least have the ability to develop – the characteristics of great leadership team members discussed in Chapter 2. These characteristics include foresight, managing complexity, having a greater good focus, and modeling values. For example, we find that most new leadership team members have sound capability to manage the complexities of running their own business units but struggle to adapt to the breadth of complexity required to lead the entire organization.

Shift Mindset. The decision to move from a senior staff model to a leadership team model is almost exclusively the decision of the CEO. Once the decision is made, a CEO must evolve how she views her role and begin to model some important behaviors to facilitate the evolution. Ultimately, these behaviors require a dramatic shift in the CEO's mindset (see insert). Leadership coach Marshall Goldsmith tells CEOs he works with that they must model behaviors they want other leaders to embrace. "If you want everybody else to do this, you go first. Let them watch you do it."[28] Creating adult behavioral changes is hard work and requires CEOs to self-reflect and commit to adopting behaviors required to help their teams become resilient, committed to learning from each other, and laser-focused on business results. Based on experience working with leadership teams in organizations across multiple industries, there are three behaviors CEOs must model in addition to modeling the values espoused by the organization.

---

28 Marshall Goldsmith, *What Got You Here Won't Get You There: How Successful People Become Even More Successful!*, (New York, Hyperion, 2007), 166.

> From having all of the answers to tapping into the collective wisdom of the team.
>
> From lead problem solver to facilitator.
>
> From refereeing and minimizing conflict to fostering productive dialogue.
>
> From managing senior staff to leading a team.

Figure 5: CEO Mindset Shift

Self-Awareness: As discussed in Chapter 6 all leaders have blind spots that sometimes hold them back from being their best as colleagues, bosses, or teammates; they think they are behaving one way while others see them showing up differently. CEOs are often shocked when they get feedback from their leadership team colleagues. To create an environment where team members proactively address their blind spots, CEOs must commit to addressing their own first. Relationships among leadership team members are strengthened when CEOs take the lead in helping team members strive to understand how others view them, so they are not clouded by inaccurate assumptions and lack of diligence.

Productive Dialogue. Productive dialogue, which was the focus of Chapter 6, is the ability for teams to challenge, debate, and discuss their most important issues in a manner that progresses the issues and leaves minimal relational scars. Unfortunately, productive dialogue is a rare practice on most leadership teams. And shutting down dialogue can happen quickly. For example, when someone's voice isn't heard, when teammates get defensive with one another, or when groupthink sets in, many teams begin to shut out dissenting views. When CEOs demonstrate that they are open to feedback, actively listen to different perspectives, and view confrontation as a natural part of the team's way of operating, leadership teams are much more likely to engage in productive dialogue.

Accountability. As mentioned in Chapter 7, great leadership teams evolve into ones where individuals feel accountable to the team, the leader serves more as a coach rather than the primary source of accountability, and the team becomes competent at holding itself accountable. CEOs must model the behaviors they expect for their team. This includes receiving feedback well as well as providing timely, direct, and respectful feedback. CEOs also need to clarify that their role does not exist to settle problems or constantly monitor the team; rather it is focused on creating an environment where peers address concerns immediately, directly, and respectfully with each other.

* * *

SIDEBAR: Loose Expectations Are Dangerous

A recent LinkedIn Learning survey of 3,000 professionals concluded that the inability to set clear and consistent expectations is hands down the most frustrating quality they have experienced with their managers.[29] In my work with leadership teams, I have witnessed first-hand the problems that ensue when expectations are unclear.

Root Causes. Lack of discipline and avoidance are two key issues that hold executives back from setting and managing clear expectations. Let's start with discipline. It is difficult to establish clear expectations when strategy and related priorities are not well-defined or when priorities are constantly shifting. I worked with one CEO who led the success-

---

29 Paul Petrone, *The "Most Frustrating" Thing a Boss Can Do Is...*, (LinkedIn Learning Blog, 2018), 1.

ful growth of his company strictly on intuition and brute force. However, once the company went public, his span of responsibility grew significantly. As a result, his team of talented individual contributors struggled: *What is most important? Who is responsible for which cross-organizational initiatives? How do we prioritize limited resources?* This caused infighting and created serious inefficiencies within the company.

Tension is a natural part of negotiating and establishing clear expectations. Unfortunately, many executives (in fact, most adults) tend to avoid tension as they simply do not like conflict, difficult conversations, or disagreement. Avoidant behavior is manifested when executive teams fail to discuss, debate, or gain clarity on the natural overlaps between their roles. For example, without clarity, faulty assumptions are often made about the obvious gray areas between product development and operations, investor relations and marketing, customer service and fulfillment, and many others. Delaying difficult or controversial discussions is another way that avoidance behavior is exhibited. When executives "kick the can down the road" about issues such as compensation, ownership, or promotions, frustration brews and trust begins to erode. I have observed CEOs destroy once productive relationships by making pseudo promises like, "don't worry, I will take care of you". There are usually good intentions behind these statements, but as time passes the expectation gap often widens (i.e., "you are only giving my X% ownership?").

Consequences. Loose expectations come with consequences. Even healthy leadership teams will exhibit signs of confusion and frustration if teammates aren't on the same page. For example, in a fast-paced environment, leadership teams will sometimes take action without gaining clarity on expected outcomes or who is doing what by when. Those on healthy teams are resilient and less likely to let confusion or frustration get in the way of what's most important; they know how to step back and gain clarity to get things back on track.

Teammates on unhealthy teams are much more likely to let their individual frustrations grow while at the same time avoiding the often-difficult discussions necessary to resolve any frustrations. Unfortunately, the longer any frustration lasts, the greater the likelihood that the impacts will be significant; such as when time and attention are deviated from what is most important, like customer service, operational efficiency, and innovation. A typical avoidance scenario unfolds like this: *Teammates avoid having tough discussions, they talk negatively about each other, they directly or indirectly undermine colleagues with whom they are at odds, the situation gets out of control, and eventually the CEO must step in to help temper the situation.* Often the issue at hand is resolved in the short-term, but the seeds of dysfunction are sown for the longer term. Trust among teammates – which is extremely hard to rebuild – is degraded. The team continues to miss important opportunities to learn how to disagree and challenge each other *productively*. Managers and staff observe how leadership team members function together, and negative behaviors (avoidance, passive aggressiveness, hiding information) tend to cascade throughout the organization.

Recalibrate. As described above, loose expectations can be dangerous for individuals, teams, and organizations; and the path to gaining necessary clarity is not always a smooth one. Acknowledging the challenges and committing to address them are important steps that leadership teams need to take to get on the road to recovery. Building an environment where leaders become great at working with each other and their teams to establish clear expectations will reduce tension and frustration, enabling all involved to maintain focus on growing, innovating, serving customers, and taking care of employees.

* * *

Chapter 8 Takeaways

1. Organizations today are too complex for CEOs to run on their own, but bringing together a talented group of senior leaders is not enough to build an effective leadership team.
2. The CEO's primary leadership team role is to establish the conditions that will help the team to thrive and to be resilient.

   a. CEOs are responsible for selecting leaders with a team mindset.
   b. CEOs must model a team-focused mindset.
   c. CEOs must help their teams to define a clear purpose.

CHAPTER 9:
A PRAGMATIC APPROACH

"The way to get started is to quit talking and begin doing."

- Walt Disney

Great executive teams never succeed by accident. It takes hard work, commitment, and patience to evolve from a collection of individual executives to a truly great team. This chapter describes a pragmatic and fluid approach for working with leadership teams to strengthen the capacity of the team along with each individual to build a *great* leadership team. The approach is developmental rather than training-focused and enables individuals and teams to learn, practice, and build both individual and collective leadership capacity over an extended period. The uniqueness of the approach is that it focuses on two distinct but interconnected components: (1) The team as a system has characteristics that transcend those of any of the individual members; and (2) The individual team members play a significant role in how the team works together to achieve a common outcome.

There is no perfect time to start building a great leadership team. However, there are a few triggers that many teams use to initiate this important work, including the appointment of a new CEO, departure of old team members and addition of new ones, and dysfunction getting in the way of results. The ideal starting point is when a new team is being launched – a new CEO or new team members – as this provides an opportunity to build a strong foundation and avoid mistakes that may decelerate progress. Most teams, however, focus on building or rebuilding leadership teams when significant dysfunction emerges – not achieving goals, team members working at cross purposes, CEO involved in too many issues. Regardless of when they start, CEOs and their leadership teams should consider the following stages as a guide for building a great leadership team: Prepare, Launch, Commit.

Prepare

As mentioned earlier, building a great leadership team requires much more than gathering the CEO's direct reports and expecting them to function as a team. CEOs are responsible for establishing the conditions that enable their teams to be as effective as possible. This starts with the structural elements described in Section One. They must select leaders who either possess or have the potential to develop the four characteristics of great leadership team members: foresight, greater good focus, management of complexity, and modeling values. They must also shape an initial purpose for the team so that each member has a strong sense of what issues they will be addressing together.

In addition to these important responsibilities, CEOs should also step back and determine if they have the disposition and skills required to build a great team or if they could benefit from additional support. CEOs are critical members of their teams, and some find it difficult to remain objective given their active involvement in the team's work. Others recognize that they might not have the coaching and team process skills necessary to build a great team. Some CEOs possess these important coaching skills and are comfortable wearing two hats so they can actively participate while maintaining objectivity. Most CEOs, however, don't meet these requirements and often seek the counsel of an experienced leadership team coach.

Securing a leadership team coach is an important but challenging decision. All coaches are not created equal; some are focused on helping individual executives to develop leadership skills and address blind spots, while others concentrate on building great teams. Both are useful resources but, when building a great leadership team, coaches should work primarily on behalf of the leadership team and possess a few important skills. First, coaches must have executive-level experience with a mindset of "I understand your challenges" rather than "do it this way." They must serve as non-biased parties with no agenda or prescriptive technical business solutions. Next, they must understand strategy and team design and dynamics, and have experience deploying an approach to building effective leadership teams. Perhaps most important, leadership team coaches must have the ability to objectively help team members get to the heart of a leadership team's challenges in a direct and empathetic manner.

Launch

Launching a leadership team is primarily about gaining agreement on important strategic, operational, and behavioral expectations. An essential first step in the launch process is for the CEO to have one-on-one discussions with each team member. These discussions should emphasize the mindset shift required to serve on a leadership team and the new cross-organizational leadership roles each member will be expected to play. Each member should also have an opportunity to share their expectations of the team, as well as the areas they believe they need to work on to become effective team members. The next step in the launch process involves work sessions where team members help the CEO further shape the team's purpose, develop team operating principles, and a cadence for progressing and monitoring priority strategic and tactical issues. During these sessions, team members begin to build trust by getting to know each other at a deeper level so they can begin to understand each other's journeys, motivations, aspirations, and fears.

The most important part of the launch stage is gaining agreement on what a great leadership team will look like for the organization they serve. Existing teams should assess how well they are performing against this ideal vision which will serve as a baseline for measuring progress. It will also help to pinpoint any structural or relational actions necessary to strengthen the team's effectiveness. The team will be encouraged to go beyond the assumptions that individuals often make and discuss and debate to gain clarity at the level of actions and behaviors. Being aligned doesn't mean that the team needs to agree on everything, but it does mean that it needs to be in sync on the vision and strategy, and that team members cannot work at cross-purposes to execute.

Commit

Commitment requires diligence, which is a careful and persistent effort that drives performance and learning. When a leadership team is diligent, they come to agreement on the processes necessary for effective team learning. The commit stage is where the hard work begins as this is where the team puts into practice the individual and collective actions identified in the launch stage. The important cycle of executing, receiving feedback, learning, and executing again is essential for helping the team maintain alignment. Challenges and disagreements will naturally emerge, and the team's ability to use these instances to build trust rather than resort to old habits of passive aggressiveness or lobbying the CEO will be tested. It won't be perfect but those leadership teams that work diligently to live up to their commitments and hold each other accountable are much more likely to move towards achieving the picture of a great team they painted.

Chapter 9 Takeaways

1. A developmental rather than training-focused approach enables individuals and teams to learn, practice, and build individual and collective leadership capacity over an extended period.

2. CEOs are responsible for establishing the conditions that enable their teams to be as effective as possible, including selecting the right team members and shaping a purpose that helps focus the team on important cross-organizational priorities.

3. Experienced leadership team coaches can be useful resources to guide leadership teams as they build strong structural and relational foundations.

4. Launching a leadership team is primarily about gaining agreement on important strategic, operational, and behavioral expectations.

CHAPTER 10:
LEADERSHIP TEAM ROLES

"If everyone is moving forward together, then success will take care of itself."

- Henry Ford

Most would agree that a great leadership team can and *should* be a powerful competitive advantage for any organization. Unfortunately, great leadership teams are scarce. Just ask employees in a lunchroom or lobby about their leadership team and you'll be met with responses like, "what team?" or "I wouldn't really call them a team but more of a dysfunctional group." And most senior executives would agree with these sentiments.

Google's seminal study to determine what makes a 'perfect team' revealed that 'to build a successful team, you must find the right balance between results and culture.'[30] Too much emphasis on results at the expense of healthy team dynamics will eventually jeopardize the team's ability to sustain results. The opposite is also true; a team that is hyperfocused on building a great culture and takes its eye off why the team exists will also hinder results.

---

30 Duhigg, *What Google Learned.*

So, what can be done to ensure that leadership teams strike this balance? It all starts with defining what it means to be a leadership team. A great leadership team has three primary roles that require members to hold each other accountable to set performance goals and a common purpose. One role is to serve as the steward for their organization's strategic direction. Another important role is to leverage the skills and experience of team members to focus on the most pressing issues facing the organization. A leadership team is also responsible for modeling and cascading desired behavioral expectations or culture throughout their organizations.

Stewardship. Effective leadership teams serve as stewards for their organizations – the board of directors, investors, and employees rely on leadership teams to set direction, allocate resources, monitor progress, and overcome roadblocks. Composed of senior leaders of diverse functions, leadership teams must work together to solve shared problems and ensure aligned action and collective responsibility for the organization's performance. Stewardship success depends on the ability and willingness of each team member to address not just their individual functional or business unit responsibilities but also their collective responsibility for the entire organization. Senior leaders are uniquely positioned to take a global perspective on the business, recognize patterns, evaluate, and assess risks and direct the organization to take necessary action. They don't need to agree on everything, but they do need to be aligned and stand behind collective decisions.

A leadership team's stewardship role requires a long-term outlook which can be challenging. From a business results perspective, great leadership teams take on mutual accountability for achievement of the strategic direction. Even in those cases where a functional leader might have limited input or influence, on great leadership teams the team wins only when key long-term targets are met, such as market share, growth, earnings, etc. Great leadership teams also recognize that, at times, their ability to subordinate functional roles to enterprise roles, engage productively with each other on difficult challenges, and treat each other with integrity and respect will facilitate their ability to effectively play their stewardship role and help cascade a positive culture throughout their organizations.

Performance. Great leadership teams have purpose beyond their stewardship role; one that leverages the collective experiences and talents of each team member. As mentioned in Chapter 3, mission and strategy should certainly strongly inform a leadership team's purpose; they do not provide adequate guidance for how the team should behave and operate as a unit. Gaining clarity on a leadership team's purpose drives consistency of approach and establishes a foundation for how the team will operate and behave as a unit. Like a leadership team's stewardship role, execution of a common purpose requires leadership teams to maintain a sometimes-challenging balance of focus on business results and productive behaviors that will influence results.

Culture. Culture is a fancy way of describing "how things are done around here." It is the accumulation of the beliefs, norms, and values shared by employees up, down, and across an organization. Culture is reflected in the behaviors and processes that are created to realize an organization's strategic direction. Leadership teams are responsible for defining and refining the values that will best serve their organizations, and they play a pivotal role in shaping and maintaining desired values. Employees take their cues from how well their leadership teams interact and how effective they are at holding each other accountable. For values to become more than platitudes and become part of the fiber of how employees operate, leadership teams must collectively and individually model these values. Most importantly, leadership team members need to hold each other accountable for living the values as a team and help each other cascade this way of operating throughout their organizations.

Great leadership teams recognize that values are not just the soft stuff but rather a critical element in achieving desired results. They view values as a potential competitive weapon as they compete for employee and management talent, strategic partnerships, and customer loyalty.

Measuring Leadership Team Effectiveness. To play the roles discussed above, leadership teams must operate effectively as a team. Great leadership teams have a strong pulse on the basic blocking and tackling factors that enable them to focus on and achieve tangible business results. The interplay between a leadership team's structural dynamics such as composition, purpose, and cadence and its relational dynamics, which are the factors that influence how team members interact, is an incredibly important dynamic that is often overlooked. When leadership teams are struggling, leaders will often take action to correct one or the other set of elements rather than look at the cause-and-effect relationship between them. Specifically, there is no doubt that insufficient structure can exacerbate relationships among team members. For example, misaligned incentive structures can inadvertently create competition that naturally puts pressure on relationships. On the other hand, bad relationships among team members can expose poor structural design as exemplified by a team that avoids debate about critical issues despite having well-planned meetings with great agendas.

A leadership team isn't just a collection of individuals; it is a living, dynamic entity with its own personality, spoken and unspoken rules, vision, blind spots, and even moods. It is because of this important context that I use Team Coaching International's (TCI's) Team Diagnostic as part of the pragmatic approach described in Chapter 9 to help measure and monitor the effectiveness of leadership teams.[31] With the Team Diagnostic, a leadership team's needs are explored independent of the needs of any single member. This shifts the attention and the work of the team members to the team itself.

The Team Diagnostic uses everyday common language to assess team performance from two perspectives: (1) What results is the team achieving? (Structure/Productivity) and (2) How is the team achieving these results? (Relationships/Positivity). The Team Diagnostic uses seven productivity factors and seven positivity factors and, through increasingly detailed layers of analysis, a comprehensive baseline is provided for taking specific action on a few important areas of improvement. From this baseline, performance can be assessed periodically from the perspective of the team itself, the Board, and team members' direct reports, among other stakeholder groups. The graphic below illustrates the specific dimensions assessed using the Team Diagnostic.

---

31 Phillip Sandahl & Alexis Phillips, *Teams Unleashed: How to Release the Power and Human Potential of Work Teams,* (Boston • London, Nicholas Brealey Publishing, 2019), 14-18.

What results is the team achieving? (Competencies that support the team's ability to be productive.)	How is the team achieving these results? (Competencies that create an environment that supports effective collaboration.)
• Resources	• Respect
• Decision Making	• Values Diversity
• Alignment	• Camaraderie
• Accountability	• Communication
• Leadership	• Constructive Interaction
• Goals and Strategies	• Optimism
• Productivity	• Trust

Figure 6: TCI's Team Diagnostic

Leadership teams can be a force multiplier for their organizations and, as the Google study suggests, teams that effectively balance a focus on business results with building a healthy and productive culture increase their organization's likelihood for sustained success. Great leadership teams bring this balance into all the work they do including serving as the steward for the organization's strategic direction, leveraging team member talent and experience to integrate on important priorities, and embedding a desired culture throughout an organization. Deploying a leadership team measurement framework that reinforces the results / values balance across these important roles will build a foundation for continual refinement and sustained success.

Chapter 10 Takeaways

1. A great leadership team has four primary roles that require them to hold each member accountable:

    a. Serve as steward for an organization's strategic direction;

    b. Focus on the most pressing issues facing the organization;

    c. Model and cascade desired behavioral expectations throughout their organizations; and

    d. Continually evaluate and improve their effectiveness as a team.

2. The interplay between a leadership team's structural and relational dynamics is an important dynamic that is often overlooked.

3. A sound leadership team measurement approach requires leadership teams to maintain a sometimes-challenging balance of focus on business results and productive behaviors that will influence results.

CHAPTER 11:
CONCLUSION

"Smooth seas do not make skillful sailors."

- African Proverb

In Chapter 1, the CEO of Metropolitan Contracting summed it up well when he said, "Why did we wait so long to get our leadership team in shape?... we are about to accomplish so much more than we ever thought was possible." He recognized that he didn't have to live with the dysfunction that was holding Metropolitan back– and neither do you. As I have mentioned throughout this book, there is no perfect leadership team. But as Metropolitan's CEO suggests, the journey to building a great leadership team can take you one step closer to greatness.

In this book I have described the structural and relational factors required for building great leadership teams and the interplay between them and have outlined a pragmatic approach for building great leadership teams. I also referred quite often to the diligence, self-awareness, and patience that team members must possess to build great leadership teams. These important skills along with the model presented in Chapter 2 are critical for helping leadership teams navigate the often-rocky path to building a great team.

Leading any organization is a challenging endeavor wrought with unexpected developments such as a pandemic, supply chain interruptions, worker shortages, new competitors, and many others. In addition to these environmental strains, successful organizations experience growing pains where growth often outpaces processes and technology and, in some cases, the capabilities of some managers and staff. In these challenging times, everyone looks to the leadership team for guidance and direction. Those teams who have done the hard work of building strong structural and relational foundations are much more likely to embrace the challenges in a manner that gets results, builds resilience, and reinforces a healthy culture.

Even the best leadership teams experience setbacks where internal and external forces chip away at the team's ability to remain positive and productive – a CEO has begun to tolerate the toxic behavior of a team member, team meetings have become painful, functional leaders have reverted to territorial behavior, etc. My hope is that this book has provided a framework and some guidance for getting leadership teams back on track after inevitable periods of dysfunction. There is no magic; teams that are experiencing significant dysfunction must step back and honestly assess where they are out of whack both structurally and relationally and then use the practical advice in this book to take action to get back on track.

Leadership should be focused on doing one thing: creating conditions where people can do great work. When a leadership team dedicates itself to being a true team, organizations accomplish more than they ever thought was possible. And in doing so, the lives of every member of the organization, as well as the lives of those the organization serves, becomes infinitely more engaging, rewarding, and meaningful.

Good luck on your journey!

Made in the USA
Middletown, DE
15 June 2022

67198169R00066